To Jane enjoy your path on the Rocket E

The Angel & the Alien:

My Psychic Adventures, Past Lives, Rituals & Lists

By Ginger

Illustrated by Adam Henson

Blessings Ginger

Goblin Fern Press

Madison, Wisconsin

Published by:
Goblin Fern Press, Inc.
3809 Mineral Point Road
Madison, WI 53705
Toll:free: 888-670-BOOK (2665)
www.goblinfernpress.com

ISBN-10: 1-59598-035-0
ISBN-13: 978-1-59598-035-9

Library of Congress Cataloging Number: 2005928057

Permissions and quantity discounts are available from the publisher.

Printed in the United States of America.

Dedication

To all my angels and guides;

To Marianne, Sara, John, and Joe,
Galen, Boye, and David;

And all the angels, named and unnamed,
who come and go.

I thank you.

Table of Contents

Foreword 1 by Dan Churchill 7
Foreword 2 by David E. Stanger...9
Introduction...11

Book 1 – Psychic Awakening

Chapter 1   The Angel and the Alien 15
Chapter 2   The Door Opens 31
Chapter 3   Beyond 46
Chapter 4   Dreams 63
Chapter 5   Reincarnation 77
Chapter 6   Animals 93
Chapter 7   House-Clearing..103
Chapter 8   Karma 111
Chapter 9   Field Notes 117
Chapter 10 The Shaman..145
Chapter 11 Healing Codes of the Universe.............................151

Book 2 – My Past Lives

The Station...167
Egypt...177
The Lions 199
Wagon Train 209
Bedouin Diary...231

Book 3 – Rituals and Lists

Introduction to Rituals and Lists..255
The 33 Levels: Upper and Lower 257
The Law of One 260
Body Healing 261

Table of Contents, cont.

Gardening with Elementals.................................... 263
Family Prayer.. 265
Removing Addictions 267
Sleep Ritual... 269
Separation Ritual.. 271
Follow-Up to Soul Retrieval Ritual 273
Visualization 275

Epilogue 277

Resources & Additional Reading......................... 281

Foreword 1

By Dan Churchill

I am a third-generation medium and spiritualist. In the mid-1860s, my great-uncle, James P. Green, founded the Vermont State Spiritualist Association. I am a life member of the American Society of Dowsers (ASD) and Vice President of the Vermont Spiritualist Association (VSA). In addition, I am a 32-degree member of the Vermont Masonic Lodge and Secretary of the Black River-Lafayette #85 Masonic Lodge.

My great-uncle, the first in our family to openly demonstrate his spiritual side, would often delight the local spiritualist association members with his ability to levitate heavy objects. Back then, the meeting halls would usually contain a grand piano for musical performances. To the enjoyment of members and visitors, Mr. Green would ask as many as ten good-sized ladies to sit on the grand piano for a levitated waltz around the parlor or hall. He would extend his hands over the front of the piano, which could weigh in excess of 2000 pounds, and it would rise up six to twelve inches off the floor without his even touching it. My mother, Mary Green, was a teenager at the time and during one performance, against her mother's wishes, she took a ride on the piano as it waltzed around the room. My mother described it as the most exciting ride of her life. Although my grandmother attended the meetings, she refrained from the piano ride as her religion could not explain how Mr. Green could do this.

I have worked with Ginger for nearly six years at the time of this writing. She has come to me with questions about issues of a spiritual nature. I introduced her to the 33 levels going up and the

33 levels going down that are available to souls who are on the other side. To my surprise, Ginger developed a map of those levels. She asked that I grade this work with my guides. I was told that the work was ninety percent correct, and while the remaining 10 percent was not wrong, some levels were known by other names for more expanded meanings. Ginger asked if she should make changes to the names and the answer came back "No." The map is reproduced in the Rituals and Lists section of this book.

During our acquaintance, I have validated several dreams for Ginger. At one Vermont Spiritualist Convention, she told me of a very colorful, lucid dream she had and asked if the beautiful Adonis who had appeared to her was someone with whom she had had a past history. I assured her he was. "I just knew that," she said, laughing, "for the memory was so vivid."

I have done over 400 spiritual readings throughout my career. Ginger is the first person who has ever reached "100" on the karma chart I use. Her response: "That just means I'm valedictorian of this class." She has also jumped from old soul-junior level to transcendental soul-junior level and back. In my experience, such jumping from level to level is very rare. My advice to her: "Whatever you're doing, keep it up!"

I am most pleased to write the foreword to this book in support of Ginger's work. Ginger has been doing readings at Vermont Spiritualist and ASD functions and is rapidly developing a following. She is continually perfecting her skills in mediumship, as well as dowsing for personal and planetary healing.

Dan Churchill
Vermont, 2005

Foreword 2

By David E. Stanger

To understand this book, one must have some belief, or at least acceptance, of the idea of reincarnation. This is a concept that has been understood by certain groups for eons, and in North America, is being more widely accepted by a large number of people. If you read this book with at least acceptance, by the time you have finished, it will begin to be at least belief. My understanding is that each of our souls has been has been in the Universe almost from time immemorial, though we may not have been on our Earth all that long. Many of us have been on our beloved Mother Earth for many, many lifetimes and have enjoyed every minute, or at least the spiritual experience of being here.

Ginger is one of those people. Sometimes she may not feel that she has enjoyed it, but when she returns to the other side, her new understanding and knowledge will be filled with joy as she digests this lifetime and looks at it with her advisors. Knowledge and understanding of reincarnation bring a great deal of peace and comfort to those who understand and welcome this knowledge. Deep within, you know that your soul is immortal, and in a real sense, you look forward to your return through the white light, as has often been described in books and articles about near-death experiences.

It is also my understanding and firm belief that we first come to Mother Earth as baby souls and progress, sometimes slowly, sometimes quickly, through young souls, teenage souls, middle-aged souls, mature souls, and old souls. Each one of these categories has many different levels. It is when we reach the "old soul" category that we are wise enough to slow down, look around and begin to realize that our assignment is to help one another and Mother Earth, certainly no small task. A bit about karma: Each time we return to Mother Earth, we bring with us "karma." Simply put, karma is what we wish to accomplish at a spiritual level while we are on Earth this time around. We have this knowledge as infants, but unfortunately, we soon forget it and spend the rest of our lives trying to find out why we are here. Others just blunder around. It seems a very strange way to "conduct business," but we cannot know all the ramifications of the plans for the Universe and "God," whoever S/He may be.

Ginger is an old soul who has returned to this Earth for very specific spiritual understanding. Part of this understanding is to give guidance and help to other souls on this Earth, so that they may live out their karmic lives in a more comfortable fashion. To do this, she has accepted her present karmic life and has used it as a tool not only to bring this book into being, but to all healing as well. Ginger has certainly found her karma and is delightfully and humbly passing it on to us. It has been my privilege to know Ginger and to read parts of her book and past lives. My hat is off to her and her life— this time around!

David E. Stanger
Founding Member of the
Canadian Society of Dowsers

Introduction

I am an angel! Don't worry. You're an angel as well. We are here on this planet Earth trying to do a good job of being human. Human has a very specific meaning in the grander scheme of things, related to the number of chromosomes and other criteria.

This book is the culmination of my years in traditional and spiritual healing, and experiencing one karmic lesson after another. I actively worked in health care for over 25 years. I established and administered a care home for ten residents, putting all my energy, time, and money into it. This was not my true path and I had to learn the lesson that I can't save the world all by myself.

Because my physical body has deserted me, I have put my energy and effort into using and developing my mind. I knew I had to write this book, to share with others many of my experiences, healing techniques, and "old soul" wisdom. I salvaged parts of an ancient computer from a church about to discard it. Then I found the "brains," a CPU, at a recycling store. Though I was unable to write, I could type, and type I did. Within seven weeks, I had written seventy-five pages, or half the book. Using the resources of the local libraries, the Community Action Center, and the Vermont Vocational Rehabilitation Center, I was able to get online, communicate with a publisher, and even received a grant to support the production of the book.

You hold in your hands, dear Reader, the physical results of persistence, will, and the support of angels here on earth and beyond. Some of my karmic lessons were great, others were unpleasant to be sure. That is all behind me now. On my contract scroll in the Hall of Records on the lower 9th level, I had written "Mystery and Adventure" for this part of my life and it is NOW that my story truly begins. Everything before is background for my life path. Many truths have been revealed to me over the course of my lessons. Let me share with you now the adventures and mysteries for which I signed on in this lifetime.

Blessed be!
Ginger
Vermont, 2005

Book 1

Psychic Awakening

Chapter 1

The Angel and the Alien

Work was going well and I had a nice business running a residential health care facility. If I worked hard for a few more years and stayed focused, I would be able to put away a little money and be comfortable. My work kept me from thinking about the past, the life I had left behind, the dreams of a family I had cherished from childhood. At that time in my life, I would work up to 72 hours non-stop. I also went to school and worked two jobs, keeping at bay the past that lurked just at the edge of my consciousness.

I had left a dead-end relationship three years before. No loss there; the guy had been a loser and had wanted me to be one, too. No way! After years before that of being in a bad marriage, that was not going to happen to me again. Near the end of a 25-year marriage to a weak, abusive alcoholic, I realized one of us was going to die. I made the choice it would not be me. No man was going to tell me what I could or could not do.

I like to dance and went out whenever time allowed. There were always a few unattached guys around, so it wasn't ever hard finding partners. I never gave my real name or any information for an ongoing relationship. My usual line was: "I don't smoke, don't drink, and don't go out with women." That summed it up and got a laugh. One night, I met a postal worker and we had a good time. He was in the area hunting with a friend. Even though I had given him no real information, I did get a Christmas card from the "The Hunter" that year. Lesson: If you wish to remain anonymous, beware of postal workers!

Whenever I was stranded because of a car problem, I had to hitchhike. The fellows who picked me up, I called my "knights of the road." One such fellow, Ted, had taken a liking to me. He used to come to my cabin and help me with all the projects I was working on. He helped me put in doors and windows, and would even bring a picnic lunch or take me to a nearby restaurant. It was nice to have the company. As it turned out, he was married. I had to make a choice one day when Ted was leaving by the front door and another guy, Adam, was coming in the back; that was just a little too close for comfort.

Then there was Larry. I had stopped at his house to purchase a stove he had for sale. We talked for a bit. He asked me to go to a dance with him. I agreed and met him at the dance site. We had a good time and I met some other folks from the area. "All in all, a very successful evening," I thought. The next Monday, at the end of the work day, I was summoned to the office. Two men in suits are sitting there. They flashed their badges at me: they were from the FBI! When they started asking questions, I thought it was a joke. They didn't laugh. It seems that friend Larry had seen one of those "WANTED" shows and thought I looked like some green-eyed, 110-pound Texas outlaw. (I liked the 110-pound part, since I hadn't weighed that since grade school). Larry had turned me in for a reward. Hey, do I know how to pick 'em or what? Anyway, the suits interrogated me. I had spent thirty years of my life in the same town, raised my family, sang in the choir, taught Sunday school, volunteered at school, food shelf, 4-H, etc. Everyone knew me. Suddenly, the FBI is questioning me. How bizarre is that?

I was a woman alone by choice, cutting my own wood, doing my own thing, not asking anybody for help. The more I thought about it, the madder I got. If I had arrived in town with some idiot guy in tow, no one would have looked twice. Because I was by myself, self-sufficient, I was somehow seen as a threat.

Needless to say, the FBI didn't lock me up. They sort of apologized, saying they had to check out all leads. It was a very good thing I didn't see "Larry" for some months; I had some time to cool off. I even found it sad and funny that a man would be that desperate for fame, money, or attention.

But despite my independence and very full schedule, I was also lonely. I had moved far into the mountains of Vermont in an effort to leave the past behind. I knew no one there and the whole support network from my previous life was gone. I had only myself to rely on.

The Spiritual Side of Cars

Even though it might have appeared that I was alone, I did have help. I remember several times when my old blue '74 Caddy was taking its last gasp of life, I would say "Little angel on my left, little angel on my right, please get me to work." Those angels were certainly there the night an enormous, lumbering beast came out of the black and rainy night: 1,700 pounds of moose, making its last stand in the middle of the road.

When the war was over, I had a fat lip, a black eye, and glass peppered all over me. I remember thinking, "Either they play country music in heaven or I'm still alive." Miracle of miracles, the old Caddy was still running. The windshield was shattered, the back window was gone, the metal top had been crushed and nestled on the seat backs, bowed like a great toadstool, bent but not broken. I drove on to work and wasn't even late! My co-workers wouldn't let me work when they saw the car. They thought I might pass out (not likely). When I could not persuade them to let me work, I turn the car around and drove the forty miles home. I had to lean sideways to see the road beyond where the windshield used to be. The Caddy was retired, for it had been mortally wounded.

Because the Caddy was now out of commission, I needed to get some brake work done on my summer car, a La Baron convertible, black with a tan interior. I took it to a garage, telling the guys that I would pick it up on my way to work Saturday night. On my way home, after driving a few miles, I noticed a shimmy in the front end. I thought I would stop back at the garage in the morning, even thought it was Sunday. At about the same place I had encountered the moose, I looked left. There went my front tire, rolling down the road ahead of me! Riding a rotor is interesting, needless to say. After coming to a lopsided stop, I resolved to take a different, if circuitous, route to work, just in case the relatives of the moose were out to get me.

On God and Religion

It's funny that I had never adhered to the church dogma. God was personal to me and could never be contained in a man-made building. He dwells in every blade of grass, every tree, every sunset and sunrise, every lake, every mountain. The songs of the birds heard while walking in a wood festooned with fallen leaves of every hue. The arcing trees above, bowing slightly in His homage. The rocks, cliffs, every waterfall and brook: that is where God is. Of that I'm certain. Even while lugging water from the river or cutting up firewood, tears would come to my eyes at the sheer beauty around me. I was, and am, blessed. I'm sure most people would find my life of solitude "crazy" by today's standards, but I have always thought of it as paradise.

Speaking of such a "heaven on earth" makes me think of the time I burned up my favorite silk nightgown in the microwave. Some days I would come home after working eighteen hours straight. The cabin would be like ice. I'd get the wood stoves going and put an electric heater in the bed. Finally I'd toss a cotton nightgown into the microwave and "nuke it" for a few minutes. I'd put on the toasty gown and crawl into bed. Four hours later, the cabin would be comfortably warm. I could do what needed doing and start the rituals of life all over again. It worked very well.

One day, though, instead of a sturdy cotton gown, I grabbed my beautiful, coral-colored, absolutely favorite, silky, soft, sexy "Olga" gown and tossed it into the microwave by mistake. I turned to wash my face and suddenly smelled something unholy. Smoke rolled out of the microwave. I flung open the door. There, in a little pile of ash, were the tiny remains of my gorgeous gown! And the smell—ugh! I tossed the plate, ash and all, out into the snow. I tried to air out the cabin while holding my nose and mouth. How could anything so beautiful stink so badly?

Years later, it became a funny story. At the time, though, the tragic demise of my beautiful gown brought tears, though part of that was due to the god-awful smell I like to wear sexy, silky things next to my skin. They make me feel like a very sensuous woman. After all the babies I had nursed, I was still strong and very surely a woman. The silky softness next to my skin reminded me of my feminine side. It was hard to find a man who could satisfy me.

I knew there was one out there. I had dreamed of him since I had been about eight years old. Finding him was a different story. I had a poster which read: "You got to kiss a lot of frogs before you find a prince." Frogs seemed to be in record numbers that year—the year I burned my beautiful, coral-colored, silky, sexy soft "Olga" gown.

The moose adventure made me feel that it was time to abandon the road and settle down as well as I could. I had been a visiting nurse, putting 60,000 miles a year on my cars. I began looking at care homes when one of my clients mentioned that she had run one for years and that I would be really good at running one, too. During the next four years, I developed business plans and hunted locations and sources of funding for such a venture. One day, I found the ideal situation: a care home for ten residents located on a private road in the country. It was perfect!

Once settled into the care home, I was able to think about other things in my life. To combat my loneliness, I started going to a book club once a week. My views certainly shocked the other members: a minister and minister's wife, several retired teachers, a gardener and a housewife, all of whom had led rather secluded lives. They floated in a world far removed. One evening, I shared that I picked up hitchhikers. After all, doesn't it say in the Bible, attributed to Jesus and his disciples? "I was a stranger and you let me in" and "I was the widow and you gave me bread." The minister replied in the affirmative, but still didn't want his wife picking up strangers.

I told the group: "When you let go of everything, it makes you free." I also shared a story of a fellow I had picked up on the interstate. He was incredulous that I, a woman, had stopped for him. He looked in the back seat. Turning to me, he said he could see why I hadn't been worried about picking him up. Tara, my Rottweiler, lay placidly on the seat. I also expressed the observation that the ones closest to you are the ones who inflict the most pain, not the stranger at the door. Yes, indeed, I brought a very different perspective to that small book club group.

The Internet and my Salvation

One evening after Book Club, I arrived home around 9 p.m., loneliness pervading my thoughts. I went online to search the personals. A few looked interesting, so I sent out a couple of e-mails. I had been putting out to the Universe that I was looking for love, for someone who fit my needs. It was May and I had been captured by spring fever, no doubt. I worked in my care home almost 24/7 with a little time off here and there, so I didn't really think there was a lot of time for anyone in my life. Well, no harm in asking.

The next day, one of the men I had contacted sent back a response. Well, that was promising. So began a repartee that was both welcome and fun, as well as fitting nicely into my schedule. June came. We decided to meet at a convention at a nearby community. The keynote speaker's address was going to be on near-death experiences in children, a topic I found very interesting. I found someone to cover for me at work and went off to meet my online friend. The night was mild and I had the top down on my sports car. Tara was in the co-pilot seat.

A wonderful feeling of adventure and freedom lifted my spirits. I arrived on campus, where the sounds of drums and chanting inoculated the darkness with mystical charm. A Native American wedding ceremony was underway. I paused to listen. People were starting to congregate near the auditorium entrance. That was where I was to meet my friend.

I entered the brightly-lit hall. My eyes were blinded by the sudden glare. I walked down the hall, trying to recall what he said he would be wearing. A tall man with a badge that read "Jack" touched my arm. My e-mail partner and I exchanged greetings as he ushered me to a seat on the bleachers. So far, so good. We talked animatedly until the speaker began. The talk was very interesting. We were deep in thought, absorbing the information, each of us making our own assessment. When it was over, we filed out with the rest of the crowd, and found a spot to sit under the stars near the drummers. There, we talked with subdued voices about what we had just heard. The night was wonderful, over way too soon. We agreed to meet for lunch the next week. Jack was retired so he was flexible. We hugged at parting, each with a nice feeling, knowing we had each made a new friend.

What developed was a weekly time out for me, welcome and stimulating. Jack and I shared an interest in metaphysical issues. Healing, in the ancient practice of shamanism, resonated with me. I also started going on dowsing assignments with him. Treasure hunts, garage sales, labyrinth building, and rock hounding helped the summer pass pleasantly.

Jack's library was extensive and he was generous in giving me unlimited access to it. I would take home a book to peruse, then we would talk about it over a meal or after a movie. In the books I was devouring, I was also finding information about things I had done as long as I could remember, since childhood. Suddenly astral travel, lucid dreaming, out-of-body experiences had names. I had never realized they were all forms of psychic awareness and that people put great stock in developing these skills.

Shaman journeying and self-healing were topics dear to my heart, and I read every book I could find on shamanic themes. After years in health care, I had great mistrust of traditional Western medicine. I have become outspoken to the point of equating social demise to the "quick fix, take-a-pill" philosophy the medical "drug pushers in white coats" follow.

One evening, while Jack was on an "inner voyage" trip out West, I decided to try the Internet again. There I found a date site that gave me six months free. Within a very short time, I was having a ball talking to three or four men at a time. I never gave away too much information since it was just for company, re-placing the social life I didn't have at the moment. I was hailed by a new man, whose typing was erratic. I had been taught proper letter writing and had no understanding of the new " 'puter jargon." My first thoughts were that the guy must be from another country. I asked if he was typing challenged and also checked out his bio. He was a bit younger then I. As it turned out, he was well educated and great fun to chat with. I told him that, in high school, I had had a fan club of boys about his age. They used to carry my books and fall all over themselves to be at my beck and call.

As our chats progressed, I laughingly told him that I would keep him in my back pocket as a "boy toy." It turned out that "Zeppo" was also a world traveler and would be gone for long periods. I was "free, white and over 21" with no committed rela-tionship. Why not?

Chatting with Zeppo was exciting and a lot of fun. It became daily and we exchanged more information. One day, he asked if I would call him. I said I would and he gave me his number. I called and a woman answered. I thought I had misdialed and I tried again. No answer! After three more tries, a guy answered and told me I must have the wrong number. I went back on-line. Zeppo was there and I told him I had tried to call and that he may have given me a wrong number. "Shit, shit, shit," he typed and gave me the right number. I dialed again. This time, he answered and hellos were exchanged. He told me he wanted to adopt me, to which I replied in the affirmative, telling him I was an orphan. He thought I was funny, and then told me he had to go, as the other guys wanted to use the phone. I sat back in my chair with a big smile on my face. Life was good!

Jack returned. We fell into the old routine. I didn't mention the new liaison, for Jack and I were friends and I was sure it would not be more. Jack was a wonderful friend, mentor, mystic, and teacher, and I was quite fond of him. Nevertheless, my heart was fast falling for another. Where I was impulse-ruled and impossibility was only something to work around, Jack was a Taurus, logical to the core. Everything had to fit perfectly in his life, and was there to be crossed out, marked off, or put into a slot. To be collected, cataloged, or pigeonholed, with no room for improvising or spontaneity. Oh, but I needed his stability. Otherwise, I might just have flown off into space and kept going.

I had learned to let go, had needed to let go. It gave me a very different worldview; I had become an adventurous free spirit. Zeppo and I continued to email (the following are exact conversations, for I saved our correspondence, just to remind myself it really happened):

Zeppo: Perin is little project 25 mill, I go to B town tomorrow for the big crap, they get 2.5 bill for new project. I'm retired old fart, semi-retired. my part on perin is 70k is big deal for me am consultant only. I leave big company years ago they still contact me. gives them warm fuzzy feeling about stuff I start up. I go diff places and mash buttons, start stuff up. power plants, semi-conductor plants etc. I don't do much am what I am.

Zeppo: read your mail if have time am curious

I typed: Thought you went to B town today didn't expect you so soon, did you fly?

Zeppo: I hate this format, I went to your home page , I need to talk to you diff way, I think I can find what you need. We can help I just not sure what you need. Sorry I'm sitting here till I hear. Your name is Ginger?

I typed: ok ok instant message on aol

Zeppo: What the hell is that? oh I know wait I have it loaded on one of these damned puters damn damn

I typed: Had to go unscrew a door handle, that's life in the fast lane/ talk later got to go feed critters back later

Zeppo: Gotcha!

I typed: Crisis afoot be back

Zeppo: Ok!!

Zeppo and I continued e-mailing back and forth. I was looking for information on installing a sprinkler system in my property and despite his extremely busy schedule (he was a consultant), he offered to help me find what I was looking for. How sweet! In addition, things were heating up. We had real names now. He was Carter, I was Ginger.

I had been working on reactivating my 12-strand DNA, using the guides offered in Barbara Brennan's book, *Hands of Light*. I learned that I was from the realm of Archangel Michael, the loving realm. When we incarnate, this DNA string, part of our physical body, is deactivated. With it goes our memory of past lives, our sojourn in the angel realms between lives, and the karmic lessons we are working on in this lifetime. All this information is stored in our bodies like computer files. We can't get to them because the pathway is disconnected. When we reactivate our 12-strand DNA, we can access more of this information. That's what I was working on when I met Carter.

Carter had to go to Boston to meet some foreign engineers who were coming for one of his projects. He chatted to me before the night's activities began.

Zeppo: I sing, they lip it.

I typed: I got to see this ! oldies, C&W, rock, What?

Zeppo: Germans sing Sinatra, Japs sing Elvis is draw who sounds worse, of course after sake and schnapps, everyone sounds like Beatles

I typed: I have to add this picture to my scenario, of you in your puter room, papers flying and you singing with a cordless mike-- that is beautiful

Zeppo: Imagine this our limo driver is black, which means I have to listen to them trying to sing Stevie Wonder and Jackson 5 and Lou Rawls, is not a pretty picture I need to go soon wash my mop takes awhile to dry

I typed: I can't wait for the next installment I shell be in stitches all night, thinking of your sacrifices in the name of progress

Zeppo: It's a guy thing is Mac's turn to sit with them all nite I did it last time being contract engineer. I get to go eat and stop for a few minutes. Then I go!!! you have a good nite if your around later bout 10-11 I give you update.

I typed: Can't wait have fun, do you have to get girls too?

Zeppo: Thanks and no girls for the boys I am engineer not pimp well not yet

I typed: I think you have a whole new meaning for Global Warming!!!

Yes, I had been bitten by that little bug. This guy was really fun. My birthday was coming up and I asked Carter to call me. He said that he would give me a message.

It was the 10th of November, the day before my birthday. I had read a book on shamanic healing in the Hawaiian *Huna* tradition. The exercise indicated that it was helpful for shamanic journey work to visualize a "garden." So that morning, I got into my special chair and created a "garden" in my mind. It had a stone wall with a lovely gate and a brick path bordered with ferns and flowers. There were myriad textures of green, interspersed with lovely blooms and shrubs of every hue, shape, and height. My "garden" had a narrow wooden bridge arching over a sparkling stream that emptied into a pool. It had a great tree with a bench beneath, and a backdrop of steep rocks contained the "garden." I sat upon the bench to survey my masterpiece.

I was my "Little Girl Self," dressed in a red plaid dress with white collar and cuffs, and my brown hair was braided. Suddenly, a black-robed figure with no face appeared before me! I gasped and uttered "Carter," and then ran from the "garden" as if the devil himself was on my heels.

As I returned to my special chair, my heart pounded, and my breath came in short gasps. I then took some deep, calming breaths. I gripped the arms of the chair for support. I sat for some time collecting my thoughts and was stunned by what had happened. Nothing had prepared me for so vivid an experience. As I sat catching my breath, I remembered the shaman saying "even if the beast bares his teeth, finish the dream." After a few more calming breaths and a quick shower, back I went. He was waiting for me. This time I took his hand.

The black-robed being took me to a wooden door with long dark hinges in the center of the rocks. The door revealed a stairway leading downward. I followed him down the stone steps and encountered my mother and father, sister and brother, all of whom had passed. Farther along, I was greeted by other relatives, who patted me on the back and wished me well. Hugs and kisses all around.

I continued on with Carter (the black-robed, faceless figure). We crossed a valley with a small stream. Ahead, I could make out a swirling ball of blinding light. "Pure energy" came to mind. As we approached, I could see a picture superimposed on the ball of light. It appeared to be a Sunday school picture of Jesus from my childhood. The light reached out and took my hand. I was told I would have the gift of healing, which I had wanted for as long as I could remember. Many times in the past, while nursing a suffering person, I had laid my hands on the person in hope that the gesture would ease the pain. Now my hands tingled and I looked at them in wonder. The quest was over. This was the message Carter had promised for my birthday.

I sat back in my chair. Everything around me seemed the same, but I was forever changed! Deep breaths heaved up from inside. I mulled over all that had occurred and reviewed everything I had felt and heard. My mind was snapping and popping from the excitement. I drifted through the rest of the day, not here, not there. Doing the same tasks as any other day, but totally disconnected from them. Later, when the work load and chores were under control, I took a break. Once again in my chair, I headed back to the "garden."

It was there, the door in the rock. I went back to "Spirit/Faerie," as I came to call it. Sure enough, it was as before. My family was there. My brother, Roger, asked me to give a message to his wife. "Tell her I love her and that she should sell the house." I was also able to find my son, Boye, who had died several hours after his birth. In Spirit/Faerie, he appeared to be about eight years old. I asked him to forgive me for taking the aspirin that had taken his life. Aspirin, doctors now know, attacks the fetus, disrupting the growth of organs. My son put his arms around my neck and said in a sweet, loving voice, "I forgive you, Mommy." I held him to me and softly cried.

I had some serious questions for Carter when next we were online.

I typed: Were you in my garden?

Zeppo: I go to many gardens

I typed: Nope that will not do.

Zeppo: have you heard of Wicca

I typed: I have a passing knowledge, they are earth worshipers

Zeppo: I have more than passing knowledge,

I typed: I have to go now

Zeppo: pat pat on head from Mother Goddess, Don't be afraid we will be nice addition to your group.

I typed: I'm not afraid, there is little I fear

Zeppo: We will talk again, I have much to tell you

I typed: Oh! and next time wear brown, neon, purple anything but black it's an image thing

Zeppo: Sorry about that, I have many things to tell you, I know you have questions your friends will help you. Are you happy?

I typed: I'm crying, why do you come to me now? I was once pretty. I have nothing for you.

Zeppo: Ginger, I would not have mattered to you then, I went through that too vanity, I am young, I am old just me. We will talk again.

Some time passed and I went back to Spirit/ Faerie to talk with my son, Boye. My sister told me he was not there; he had gone to reincarnate. He had waited 31 years to give me the message of forgiveness and now was ready to move on. Later, I was to learn the next steps in his journey. I also met my sister, Winnie. She had died at the age of eight, years before I was born. Why was she still in Spirit/Faerie after almost 58 years, I wondered.

I needed to understand all this and needed to talk to someone. It was high time to bring Jack into the loop. I needed his logical earth wisdom to navigate this new maze. Because of our friendship, I also wanted to spare his feelings, for I knew that some of what I would tell him was going to hurt. I called and asked if I could come over. He said sure and that he would make lunch for us. I thanked him and drove over.

When I arrived at Jack's house, the story about the "garden," about Carter, about Spirit/Faerie, spilled out almost before I got in the door. He listened and then asked a few questions. How had I met Carter? What were more of the details about the quest and other things I had experienced? Then he took me into his office library. We looked for some books that might help explain or validate issues. I was so grateful. Jack had listened without judgment. I knew the words might have hurt him at times, and I told him he was the best friend I had ever had as I hugged him. I expressed my gratitude for his being there for me as well as I could, and told him that I would be there for him as well. With that, our relationship changed from potential lovers to mentor and student.

As I learned and experienced the new worlds that opened up to me, there were many times that I could not have handled the power, the gift, without his steady head, his guiding influence. I later learned that he had been my teacher in a past life, and that our feelings for one another were defined as just that in this lifetime as well.

The door had closed on the world as I had understood it.

Chapter 2

The Door Opens

Suddenly life was a rocket ride. No limits. No walls.
Everything that was fantasy is real and reality is dream.

Inamorata

My lover comes to me at night
Departing with the morning light
He whispers softly in my head
His touch—magik sublime
He uses mint and oil so rare
Massages gently away my care
Lie still, he speaks,
Let scenes unfold, fantasy and ecstasy
Take hold, tantra, kama sutra fare
Time—infinite to hold
My body song is heard; only he can read the words
The universe ordained
I, the Mother Goddess, lain
Gently for his ministrations, am reborn
To the earth, I give rejuvenation
My lover comes to me at night
Departing with the morning light.

I had given up television years ago as a mind-numbing bore. Now
I realized that most people are held captive by this technology.
There is a world to feel and explore. Ordinary reality and non-
ordinary reality are current expressions. The mind is the transport.
The average person uses around ten percent of his or her brain,

meaning that 90 percent goes unused. That untapped system holds the key to the Universe. Every person has the potential. Few choose the path to enlightenment. Just as a bodybuilder exercises to create more muscle, a psychic bulks up brainpower.

I went to my "garden" regularly. From there, on quest (referred to as "journey work" in the shamanic venue), I met first a bear, to whom I offered a piece of salmon. Further along on my journey, a snake appeared. I put the snake in my pocket. Finally a great bird of prey, a hawk, sat high up in a tree. I asked many questions. The answers were given to me in a dream:

> *I was working in my barn. I looked in one corner and saw a great brown bear, fur all glossy and thick. He lay asleep. The bear is my power animal and I was not afraid. I honored him and turned back to my work. I was cleaning my buggy. The top was raised. I was affixing the side curtains with buttonholes that lined up with knobs on the top. I suddenly felt a rough hand grab my shoulder. I thought my bear was behind me. I tried to turn. Two men had come up; their intent was to attack me. Suddenly, my power animal was with me. The men took one look at the huge beast. The bear, on his hind legs, teeth bared, was an imposing sight. The would-be attackers turned tail and ran..*

I understood this message to mean that my power animals would protect me.

The Black Robes

I was in the "garden," my Little Girl Self beside me. I thought about the shamanic journey books I had read; most describe climbing up rocks to reach the higher realms. Well, I had rocks behind the bench at the edge of the "garden." "Let's try it," I thought. Little Girl and I approached the rocks. We found hand holds and began to climb, hand over hand. The higher we climbed, the thicker and denser the clouds became. We traveled beyond the cloud cover. There, in a billowy landscape above the clouds, an angel greeted us. The angel said she was my sister and explained that I had come from the angel realms to incarnate on earth. I was from the realm of Archangel Michael, the loving realm. During this exchange, two other angels were seen. They were working or digging to one side of us.

Once back in the "garden," I pondered all I had been told. Life was taking on a new dimension. The more I learned, the more I needed to know and understand. I didn't even know the questions to ask.

Outside the "garden" that night, it was a full moon. I sat in my chair in the "garden." Before me appeared eleven black-robed figures. They showed me pictures of people I was working with in my business dealings. I couldn't figure out what the figures were trying to tell me. A tall, blond man came to stand before me as I sat on my bench in the garden. He was speaking, but I couldn't understand what he was saying. Then a man with long, wavy hair approached. Still, I could not grasp what they were saying to me. I had expected them—or someone. Carter had said he was teaching that night and had told me he would be thinking of me. So here they were—black-robed figures making contact with me.

By the end of their visit, the Black Robes were able to communicate with me, speaking directly into my head through telepathy. (This happens when a brain-to-brain morphic field is created). The morphic field is like a path in the woods. The more times it is used, the deeper the groove and the easier the path is to navigate. Telepathy! This is cool! The Black Robes told me they had worked with me as a child. Yes! I remembered; when I was young, I had had friends that no one else could see.

Carter and Telepathy

Carter was telepathically connected to me. He would ask me if I could feel his presence. We still chatted online, but it was also as if he were wrapping an energy field around me. I could feel a feather caressing my skin. I could feel, but hardly describe, the flow of energy he generated. Carter wanted me to contact a friend of his, "Hecate." He said she could be trusted and felt she could help me in my search for understanding. I was way too vulnerable. I read Hecate's online profile: 5'6", blue eyes, black hair, two years younger than Carter. I saw red.

To Carter, I posted: "You don't know women very well." But I agreed to e-mail this intruder into our lives and e-chatted with Hecate. We exchanged information. She wanted to watch a video. I e-mailed Carter that I had made contact and wrote truculently that I couldn't force her to talk to me.

Carter was to come to my area on December 6. When the day arrived, a heavy snowstorm had blanketed the landscape with eight inches of snow. Driving was treacherous. All day, I had alternated between wanting him to come and hoping he was safe at home. He didn't show. The next day, I hailed Hecate.

I typed: What happened? Did Carter get lost in the snow?

Hecate: No! I kidnapped him.

I typed: Such is life. I hope you got a good ransom. I hear he has bucks.

Hecate: He may, but that is not what I'm after.

I typed: Ah, yes! The mind. That should go for a good price. Just make sure you turn him upside down and shake the keys to the realm out of his pocket. Don't bother to give him your phone number; he won't remember it anyway.

Hecate: I was not talking about his mind. I want the rest of him. Oh! I forgot. I already have that. He may not remember my phone number, but he knows where I live.

I was devastated: That Carter had betrayed me was bad enough, but hearing it from "the other woman" was unconscionable on his part. My claws came out. I sent one last e-mail to Hecate, one witch to another:

I just discovered Forrest Spirit has been coming to my garden regularly. Wavy hair to his shoulders, drop-dead gorgeous. He has some moves that Carter hasn't picked up yet. I have it from sources that Carter will be gone in six months. Since you like my seconds so well, I'll train Forrest Spirit and give him to you. What are friends for? I want all my children to have pleasure. Blessed Be!! Mother Goddess.

I shed some tears and called Jack. He was more than happy to have me to himself again. I thanked him for helping me cope.

Things in the "garden" were moving along. The full moon ushered the Black Robes back. I was sitting on the bench with my Little Girl Self. Tears streaked her cheeks. She was inconsolable. I told the robed figures to go away. "Can't you see she's crying?" They left.

The next night, in my "garden," I swam in the beautiful garden pool. I could breathe under the water. I held the fish in my hands as the underwater plants swayed with the flow of the water. It was a very relaxing place to be. I stepped naked from the pool. The robed figures appeared, this time wearing brown. I walked amidst them as I expressed my apologies for sending them away the night before. I reached the center and they moved in on me. Each drew a small blade from beneath the robes. They began to stab me until I was bloody from head to toe. I felt no fear, no pain. They placed me on a pyre and burned me. Then they spread my ashes on the ground among the flowers.

I knew I had been ritually reborn. I asked my guides and power animals if this had been a good thing. They agreed it was. Jack had some reservations.

A new figure appeared in my life. He was very ethereal. He said his name was Roger, but I called him Sam. My brother's name had been Roger and I felt uncomfortable calling this being that. Sam wore dress slacks and a shirt with rolled-up sleeves. He would lean against the wall in my bedroom, sit in my car, or go to restaurants with me. When I told Jack about Sam, Jack called him an "observer." Whatever! When I offered food, he would reply that he didn't eat. I knew that I would get into trouble if other people hear me talking to him. Sam and I were a team.

I visited Spirit/Faerie, the world in my "garden," whenever I had time. I just couldn't get enough of this new dimension. There was so much to learn, understand and experience. It was almost Christmas. Little Girl Self and I decided to go to the angel realms again. We climbed the rocks and soon were there, among the clouds. My sister angel greeted us and asked Little Girl Self what she wanted most. Little Girl Self said, "I want my prince back." The angel pointed off to the right. There, on a beautiful white horse, came Carter. He took Little Girl Self up before him and rode away. I waited. They returned. Little Girl Self was so happy to have her prince back. I thanked my sister angel and asked if I might come again. She assured me I could, and told me that I was something of a legend. Apparently, many angels had incarnated because of my adventures. I'm not sure if that was good or bad. But what do I know?

The next day, Carter e-mailed me, "You win." That night, he came into my dreams and made beautiful love to me. I was so happy to have him back, nothing else mattered. As we lay side by side, I told him I knew he was coming. The angel had foretold his return. (Damn, that angel's good!) It was the beginning of a relationship of telepathic and empathetic dream sharing. Carter would speak into my left ear, infusing my mind with the feelings of love. These feelings were so intense that we would climax together. When we lay cuddling afterwards, I was amazed that my loins were dry. I pondered this for a long time, for months.

I chatted to him on the Internet:

I typed: *You're marvelous. What do you call that?*

Carter: *You mean my "shy guy 'puter program?"*

I typed: *Yes, that's it. If we could bottle it, all war would cease. We could save the world.*

Carter would come and chase me around the house. He even got me drunk one night. Seriously! Just like ET and the frogs in the film. I'm not totally clear on how it came about. All I can say is that as we were dancing around, I began to feel lightheaded. I have only been drunk once in my life, but I knew what I was feeling was like that. I had had nothing to drink. But there I was, staggering and giggling. I ended up curled at the end of my bed in a ball. He was so bad. But it was funny. I told Carter I wanted to be as strong as he was, wanted to be able to do what he did.

I could feel when Carter was with me. The two fingers on my left hand, the ring finger and the little finger, tingled. Sometimes it was really painful. One evening, I was at a Danville chapter ASD meeting, where we had broken into small groups. David Stanger, who wrote one of the forewords to this book and is the founding member of the Canadian Society of Dowsers, was leading the group I was in. We were discussing different ways of dowsing. David mentioned finger dowsing and I told him about my tingling fingers. He explained that they had been cut off in a past life. I told David that my fingers would go numb whenever my lover was with me. David expressed his thoughts about the relationship, wondering if it was a good one or not. Then he stopped abruptly, saying: "Whoa! He is strong. OK, OK! This is not our business." I went to find Jack and tell him what David had said.

Dan Churchill, a third-generation spiritualist and medium, who also wrote one of the forewords for this book, was there along with Jack. Dan said, "Yes, I can see him cutting off your fingers." He continued, explaining that Carter and I had had 129 lifetimes together. It was also Dan who explained to me about the 33 levels going up and 33 levels going down. Dan also introduced me to my primary guide, Marianne. Marianne is a sergeant in the angel army. She has 56 angel guides, first-rank (privates), in her charge. I have asked her many times if I could give her a reference; she deserves a promotion for all the help she has given me. She said she wanted to stay with me.

It was Marianne who sent me to the "Dream" website, where I offered free dream analyses and helped further develop my interpretive abilities. Marianne continues to help me with readings I do for people, and to focus at shows and fairs where hundreds of people are milling around where I sometimes do up to twenty readings in a ten-hour period. That really takes focus! She has never failed me. It was she who assured me Carter was the one for me. She told me he was a walk-in who had traded places with a little boy of four who had lost his mother.

Once, I asked Marianne if the finger thing meant that I had to cut off Carter's fingers in this lifetime. You know, that old "eye for an eye" thing. She said yes. I asked if we could commute the deal into something positive. It was actually a "High God Law," she explained, and it would have to be taken under advisement. (Obviously, there are lawyers in heaven.) I waited a few days for the decision. Carter was beside me when the answer came down. I was allowed to commute the issue to a positive action. I said "Great! He can teach me something good."

Carter piped up, "I'll teach you to spell!"

There was another "High God Law" that I asked my angels to make a request about. I'm always trying to change the world. That request had to do with my children, and is too personal to go into in this book. I was a mother asking to help her children and for that reason, the request was granted after due deliberation.

Marianne talks into my right ear, Carter into my left. Archangel Michael talks into the top of my head, which relegates me to the back corner. One time, Carter was angry about something Marianne had said. "I'm going to stuff you down a well," he said to Marianne. She returned with a "You're full of shit, Carter!" I piped up: "Hey, guys! I'm in the middle here. You're supposed to be angels and masters. How are you going to keep me on the straight path if you behave like this?" They stopped.

Sometime later, the Grandfather, who appears in another chapter, answered this dilemma: "If we were perfect, we would be on the 33rd level." Grandfather was close to that ultimate place, as he was on the 30th level.

Carter said he loved me. I returned the feeling. It was January; we had two weeks of bliss. Carter e-mailed me that he was still with Hecate, and said he may have misled me. Hecate had gone on vacation and he was missing her. His story was that was why he had said the things he had to me. Sam, the observer, was directly in front of me. I was so angry: I shape-shifted into a lioness. On my hind legs, I ripped my extended claws through Sam, goring him from shoulder to knees. I stalked around and around in the "garden," snarling and hissing, tossing my head in rage. I gradually became aware of another lion in the "garden." He was taking care not to move too close to me. My anger abated some. I slowed my pace. Finally, panting and exhausted, I dropped to the ground. The lion approached cautiously. He licked my face and nuzzled my fur. He was careful not to be too aggressive. We mated as lions will. I left the "garden," returning to this dimension.

The next day, I apologized to Sam. "That's OK," he said. "I don't bleed." I told Sam to tell Carter that I would only mate with the strongest lion in the jungle. Sam and I both laughed. That day was the turning point. I still don't know if the whole Hecate thing was made up so that Carter could tell if I really loved him. I accused him later of playing "chutes and ladders" with me, and he admitted to doing some really dumb things.

I understand now that even Carter didn't understand the full meaning of twin flames, of dual souls, the power of our connection. He thought he would be teaching me. Little did he or I know how powerful a creator I am. I took him where "angels fear to tread." Oh, well, that's life. Expect the unexpected.

From that moment in the "garden" on, Carter never left my side for more than a day. I would feel his presence at 4 o'clock in the morning. We would make love until 7, when I had to start my day. When I would take a break before lunch, he'd be there. At 9 in the evening, when I finished my day, he would be waiting for me. If I stayed away too long, he would rattle the pipes to let me know he was getting impatient.

I finally e-mailed: "Are we married?"

If Carter had other women, I didn't care. He was with me all the time. It was heaven, tantra, kama sutra! It worked for me! He never stopped until I was totally satisfied. I knew I pleased him, too. That "shy guy 'puter program" was magnificent. I kept advocating for the evolution into a physical relationship. That was the only one of the five senses we had not yet explored. Carter gradually weaned me from the "garden," which was a starting point to another dimension. I didn't need it anymore. I could make transitions ad-lib. It was like being Disney's cartoon character, Dumbo, with his magic feather; even when he lost the feather, he could still fly. And even though I no longer needed the "garden," I still liked to swim in the pool, play with the fishes, and roll naked on the soft grass. In the "garden," I could feel and see Carter.

One Friday night, Carter came to the "garden." I was having a hard time understanding his words as he stood naked before me. I realized he was drunk when he passed out on the ground of the "garden." I didn't know what to do. I called to Sam. I manifested a blanket and put it over Carter. I came out of the "garden" and asked Sam if there was anything else I could do, and if Carter was going to be all right staying there all night. When I returned later to check on Carter, he was gone.

He did return, unscathed from his "garden" adventure. I observed that maybe the Friday three-martini lunches needed to be reevaluated. I pleaded for him to come to me in the physical. One night, he sent me so much of himself that I could touch his body, feel the texture of his skin as he lay beside me. He felt warm, under a sheen of perspiration. I fell asleep, holding him in my arms. I was shocked to find he was not there when I awoke.

Another time, I asked my power animal to guide me to Carter. We set off into a wooded area, then passed through a field with high grass. We were moving very fast and everything flew past at great speed. Soon we were over water. The lights of a city appeared up ahead. Then a house. Then a bedroom with a king-sized bed. Carter lay in the middle, all wrapped in sheets. I swooped down to him and put my hands on his skin. Suddenly bells rang and dogs barked. I was instantly out of there. I'm not sure if he was hailing my arrival or warding me off. It was months before I went there again. I think the unexpected noise scared me away. Carter may have had a protective barrier up. I'm not sure if we ever talked about that experience.

In February, a fellow named Jim asked me to lunch. I accepted. Right away, Sam got all kinds of upset. "Hey, it's just lunch," I told him. "I don't get that many offers. What's the big deal?"

Sam said, "Well, what if he falls in love with you?"

I replied, "It's just lunch. Carter, what do you say?"

"I won't interfere," said Carter. What could he say, he had promised to take me to dinner way back in November. I was still waiting for that meal.

So I went to lunch with Jim. We had a nice time. Jim asked if I would meet him for lunch again the next week. I said I would. He then asked me to an Alan Jackson concert. I hadn't gone to a concert in years and told him I'd love to go. All the arrangements were made.

That night in the "garden," I said, "Now Carter, don't do anything naughty. I love you. I just want to go to this concert. Please?" I took my heart out of my chest and gave it to Carter, stating with a firm, loving voice, "You have my heart. I love only you." Carter was totally caught off-guard. He stood for a moment, amazed. Then he handed me his heart. It was our first marriage ceremony.

The day of the concert arrived. Jim and I were going to dinner first and would then catch a bus to the concert venue. The weather was cold and snowy. The roads were drifted with snow already, with no sign of letting up. Jim came for me in a nice, new, four-wheel drive Chevy "pick'em up" truck. We chatted comfortably for the forty miles to the place for dinner and bus stop. Another part of me was remembering the dream I had the night before. My face was awash in colors and I seemed to be lying down. Suddenly, a pair of eyes focused on my face, animal eyes with malevolence in them. On the physical plane, I was chatting with Jim about irrelevant matters, the truck, his day, the weather. We were deep in conversation. Dinner was great. We had to rush to catch the bus that was waiting just behind the restaurant.

We climbed aboard and found our seats without a hitch. Once at the concert, we waited for the line to dwindle and then found our seats about halfway down on the right. They were good seats with a clear view of the stage. Sara Evans appeared first. Then the stage was transformed. Large video screens were raised on either side of the stage. I immediately recognized the lights on the stage from my dream. I looked into my lap. A cameo appeared there, about a foot in length. In the middle of the cameo was Carter, with his back to me. His hair was slicked back. He was wearing a white jumpsuit with gold trim. The whole scene was washed in an eerie, bright light. Carter turned to me and there were the eyes I had seen in my dream animal eyes. Carter reached his arms up to me. He invited me to come and dance with him in the "garden" and of course, I went. How could I resist such an invitation from the man I love?

There I was, part of me sitting at the concert with Jim, the other part dancing in the "garden" with Carter. His "garden," however, was very different from mine. The dimension was strangely lit, without an evident source of illumination. It was like being in a watercolor painting, with blended shades and muted colors. It felt as if I had stepped into the painting and danced there joyfully with Carter. How strange and wonderful my life had become. Who said there was no magic, no adventure? Well, I was living proof of both.

The concert was fantastic in many ways. The ride back home was difficult, since the snow was still coming down. It was beautiful but treacherous. Jim was a good driver, but we still had to crawl along because of the road conditions. It was three in the morning before we got to my door. Jim still had 39 more miles to go to reach his place. I thanked him for a wonderful night. He didn't know just how wonderful it had been. We parted as friends. I managed to be busy when he called again. Gradually, he stopped calling. Carter was very attentive. I didn't see how he could have other women. There was just no way he could spend all the time with me and have other women. His tenderness and skill were unbelievable. He was so precious to me. He would hold me and caress me. This was the love I had dreamed of all my life. I knew married couples that had lived together for years and never spent this much time together. Carter and I would talk and play, totally engrossed in one another, no TV, no distractions. Carter had started massaging my mind. Until then, we had been engrossed in our bodies (ethereal, not physical) and our pleasure.

Now he realized that my mind needed attention as well, for I was under tremendous stress. I asked him to put himself in my place, to think about how he would feel given the circumstances of our relationship. He admitted he would have been totally unable to cope. He said this relationship was a first for him. He knew when he learned my real name, as opposed to my screen name, that I was his life partner. He had no idea how he was going to explain that to me, let alone get me to love him or even have a relationship. He didn't know that I had been intrigued by him from the first. Forces even he didn't know about had already started my path to enlightenment. I had, in fact, been searching for him since about the age of eight, when the lucid dreams, the past-life experiences, had started. I had lived with Carter before; you will read more of our experiences in future chapters.

Chapter 3

Beyond

C arter came one night, wearing his black robe. He took my hand and pulled me out of my body. He tossed me a black robe as well and said, "Put it on." Carter took me to the 30th upper level, where we met the "Grandfather." That is how Carter addressed him. "Grandfather" wished me to call him this as well. I was my Little Girl Self on this visit. (Every time I enter a new arena, I do so as my Little Girl Self. It may be so for others as well. This may be the reason that Jesus said, "You must enter the kingdom of heaven as a child." All I can say is that this is what happened to me).

Carter is an advisor to the Counsel, whose members are all from other galaxies. Each has a very important role. I knew I was in exalted company. It was very humbling, so I was quiet, attentive and apparently, made a good impression. They asked Carter to bring me back to visit anytime.

You may wonder how I knew where I was. The section of Book 3 is a chart of the spiritual levels that I created for a workshop to help myself and others understand this system. The chart serves as a road map, an index. Dan Churchill checked it for me. He said it was ninety percent correct and that the other ten percent were not wrong, but that other names could be attached. It was his information about the levels that got me to ask, each time, what level I was on.

The next time I visited the "Grandfather" with Carter, I made a joke. I pictured a soccer field with a team of neatly dressed young, male athletes, kicking the ball around. Onto the field stepped an old peasant woman in a kerchief and boots. She unceremoniously tossed the young athletes off the field, standing with her gnarled hands on her hips. In no uncertain terms, she told them, "Now I'll show you how this game is really played." I'm going to let you think about that. In any case, the Counsel thought it was a great joke.

I asked one of the Counsel members how it was that they could all be in the same room. It appeared they had different atmospheric needs. He graciously showed me. They all wore black robes. Under his robe, he wore form-fitting outfit in a medium shade of blue. I didn't know what the material was, but the word that comes to mind is neoprene, like something divers wear, only much more hi-tech. It seemed to fit his body like a second skin. There were discrete tubes that handled body functions. He was very charming in his explanations of the whole apparatus. The kind being who showed me his suit had the head of what looked to me like a fish. He walked upright and I didn't detect a tail. His galaxy was far out beyond ours.

I was invited to his planet, near a distant star. The being explained to me that they were dealing with a crisis. (I don't want to call him a "fish head"; some in this area of the U.S. might mistake my meaning as "PHISH"-head, an enthusiast of a well-known local band). The planet his "people" inhabit, remarkably, was mostly water. However, the water was slowly drying up. The beings of this planet (I would love to give you the name, but its spelling I can't match, something like ZHGAIHIFOAI), were desperate to find a hybrid being that could exist in the water and on the ever-increasing landmass. My thought was something reptilian, of course. They were seeking a more highly evolved creature, however, than most reptiles. I certainly don't want to offend any reptilians out there, but this is what I was told. My visit to this far planet was thus arranged. I went with my Counsel being. Carter didn't come with us.

I really don't want you to get the impression that this story is science fiction. Please remember that in my childhood, putting a man on the moon was just an idea. Most of us, whether we know it or not, have lived on other planets. When I do readings, I can tell how many lifetimes on earth and other planets a client has had. That being said, let's return to the adventure.

The trip to the far planet happened in the blink of an eye. How can that be, you might ask. My physical body didn't undertake the trip. My ethereal, or astral, body, with the help of the Counsel being, was transported to the distant galaxy. At first, the planet appeared round. As we approached, though, closer inspection revealed vast oceans. As I had been told, landmasses were beginning to erupt from the oceans. These land areas were covered in jungle-type vegetation. When we arrived, my guide took me to an underwater city that was quite remarkable. The beings that inhabited this city were, indeed, fish-like. Smart fish! They had created a wonderful biosphere and cultivated a food supply. Water purification plants maintained a constant supply of clean water. I didn't ask if it was fresh or salt. The information given to me now is that the water was salt. I was becoming exhausted. There was just so much to see and absorb. I was escorted back home and asked to repeat the visit whenever I could.

I had a dream shortly after this adventure. The dream was colorful and lucid. I was at a party. The people attending were family, friends, and strangers—hundreds of people. I was passing platter after platter. The platters I served were silver with handles at both ends. The silver platters were piled high with slices of a white meat. The partygoers would empty one platter and I would take up another. This went on and on. I didn't understand what was happening at that time, but would shortly.

My next visit to the 30th level was undertaken at the summons from the "Grandfather." There were about fifteen members of the Counsel in attendance, all dressed in their black robes. Each one spoke about concerns for the separate galaxies represented. Population issues were paramount. The Counsel members were dealing with what I have coined "techno-elitist destruction." You know what I mean. We have it on Earth. In our rush for "progress," we are destroying our very planet. Well, we are not alone in this issue. From what I was told, it is a universal concern. After each of the members had spoken, the "Grandfather" asked me if I would be willing to help in this crisis. My answer was immediate and affirmative, "What can I do to help?"

At first, I was asked to incarnate on the different planets. I was willing, but that wasn't practical. It would take eons. The crisis was more immediate than that. Then the idea of cloning was raised. This method would allow cross breeding to find an appropriate being for each planet's different needs. It was decided that I would donate stem cells. Each of the members of the Counsel came up and shook my hand. I gave hugs. They seemed surprised and happy at my response. There remained one figure in the back that had not greeted me. I looked at him as the others turned to one another. The black-robed figure sat in a chair with his legs crossed. It was Carter.

Carter took me home. On the way back, I said, "That was the dream."

"Yes," Carter replied.

"The platters of meat were pieces of me. I was giving myself away," I thought.

Carter said, "I knew you would do it. You didn't even ask for money."

"Well, gee, why would I ask for money?" I asked, continuing, "Look, Carter, if you think I should get something, you deal with it. I'm not interested." Personally, I thought being asked to help was a great honor.

Energy Work for Peace

I was doing a lot of energy work at that time and had read about the crystalline merkaba that encircles the earth. The angel stationed there can focus energy and send it anywhere on the planet. This energy brings love and light to the world. "I can do that," I thought so every day, from my own front porch, I would take some time to transport myself to the crystalline merkaba. The first angel I met there was Ariel. I asked her if she would help me send love to the Middle East. She agreed and together, we sent love and light to the war-ravaged area. "This is great," I thought. "I can be here at home, and help bring peace to the world. Awesome!"

The next day it was "I Am" who greeted me on the crystal-line merkaba. I admit I had to ask the name twice. The name "I Am" evoked the thought of Biblical reference and surprised the heck out of me. The angel "I Am" was happy to help me send energy to the dark places of the Earth. Each day I would meet the angel on duty and send the energy to the world's dark areas. This went on for some weeks.

I was becoming dizzy after these repeated visits and thought I was coming down with something. Since my way of dealing with illness was to drink lots of fluids and work up a sweat, I didn't curtail my energy work. It was Jack who brought to my attention that I needed to stay out of the channel. This meant that when I was sending energy, I must not send my own supply of energy. Since we beings have a limited quantity of this energy, I needed to focus universal energy, not my own meager supply. It was a little too late for that. I had already sapped my own strength. After giving away my energy to "save the world" for so many days, I was forced to stop this energy work for a time.

Another day, as I sat on the porch in my usual chair, Archangel Michael spoke to me. "You can't save the world all by yourself!" He kissed my cheek, telling me, "You have the sweetest smile, but you're so hard-headed." He continued, "One of the lessons you're here to learn is that you alone cannot save the world."

That same night, Carter came. He wanted to take me to the Counsel and to "do that heart thing," as he put it. Marry him before the Counsel. I was so weak he had to almost carry me. Carter held me up as I took the heart from my chest, gave it to him and promised my unconditional love and commitment. I started to feel faint. I left almost as soon as the words were out of my mouth.

The next afternoon, Carter told me to hurry up and come downstairs. He had a surprise for me. There were the Counsel members. They were dressed in light blue robes and each was accompanied by a mate. They were giving me a reception. I was deeply honored. I don't know if you can understand this. We are talking the 30th level here. I went down a receiving line, shaking hands and hugging and kissing these beings, in their light-blue robes.

The reason that Carter had been so insistent that I show my unconditional love and commitment to him before the Counsel was because, on a previous visit, "Grandfather" had asked me if Carter was taking good care of me I had explained to "Grandfather" that I did not think that Carter had my best interests at heart. I still had reason to believe that he was playing "chutes and ladders" with me, for he still had not come to me physically. Perhaps I was being a bit vindictive, but I knew he was playing games with me, for he would tell me to meet him somewhere and then not show up. I had told the "Grandfather" that I was going to tie Carter to a tree, turn out his pockets, and send him back. Having heard these words from me, I suspect they may have chided Carter a bit.

It is time to tell you a little of the Counsel. I have described "Grandfather" and the being with the head of a fish. The other members will best be described as humans at different stages of evolution, and can be called Grays, Reptilians, and Pleiadeians. Some have tall, willowy bodies with large heads and long fingers. Some are very small. Others were noticeably tall. (A friend and I were talking about the look of aliens—not a word I like to use. She made the comment that the lack of hair made them seem less attractive. I assured her that what she was commenting on were suits they were wearing, not the way they actually looked.)

You may be thinking that all this space stuff seems unrealistic. Other enlightened persons can validate my observations. I tell only of my experiences, and am not trying to convince you of anything. Convincing someone with a closed mind is a wasted effort. Once you try, you have lost. I sometimes use the analogy of the computer screen. An object appears, to our accepted form of reality, to be solid. Science, however, tells us differently. The supposedly solid object is ninety percent air (the new paradigm calls it "dark matter"). The other ten percent is comprised of fast-moving particles. These particles are in constant motion. Does this sound like a solid object to you? I only make this observation to loosen your perception of reality.

The Universe is a vast chessboard with players directed by conceived rules. There are no winners and there are no losers, in the Game of Life. This is a free-will zone. We incarnate with a soul group, with the group playing different roles in each of our separate lifetimes. Our souls alternately incarnate as male and female in subsequent lifetimes. The lessons we learn (karma) are listed on a contract that is stored in the Hall of Contracts. We sign before choosing our parents and birth time. Everyone knows the rules before the game starts. Then, to level the field, all memory of this contract is erased from our minds when we are born. That is the condensed version.

Before I shared this information, I had to consult my spirit guide to know if it was appropriate. I got the go-ahead, so here you have it. I have read that as many as 19,000 individuals may make up a soul family or group. That is mind-boggling. In this lifetime, 98 percent of the people I meet are known to me from other lifetimes. I give you this insight to help you understand that the star beings we meet in other galaxies are souls just like us. They wear different bodies. We ourselves have worn those same bodies in past lives. I have had 475 lifetimes on other planets. The entire span of a single soul can extend over a thousand or more lifetimes.

I present this information to you to explain my ability to encounter other world beings at will. These beings are not strangers to us. We have known them in many forms. I once asked Carter if he was a visiting dignitary from another galaxy. He replied, "Funny you should ask." I asked my spirit guides if Carter and I could pass to the next dimension together. I got no answer. I repeated the question to the Counsel. This time "Grandfather" told me that Carter was more advanced than I. I would have to work very hard in this lifetime to acquire the knowledge necessary to "catch up." It is a challenge I accept.

One of the greatest things for following my path has been the Internet. I have found more and more sites with a wealth of information. Day or night, a whole library was at my fingertips. So much information, all I had to do was ask the right questions. That proved harder than it sounds.

Some time ago, I visited a website called "www.AstralSociety.com." Many of the "regulars" had been there, attempting astral travel for the first time. They wanted to meet galactic beings. I offered to help them in this effort and took a group of about six, before giving their names to the Counsel. I admonished them to be fearless. The biggest deterrent to their efforts would be fear; fear was preventing them from astral travel and out-of-body experiences. Fear is what causes people to react instead of act. I didn't want the group of six to insult my friends or inadvertently distress the members of the Counsel, for whom I have great respect. Two of six did make contact, though it took longer than expected. The Counsel had more pressing matters to deal with at the time. Making contact with Earth-beings is a plan the Counsel supports. As Earth-dwellers evolve to the next dimension, more will be able to connect to the other realms. That is the God plan.

The project engineer for Planet Earth has determined that now is a good time for the population to move to the next higher evolutionary level. One of the consequences of this shift will be the loss of the "fight or flight" response; the fear response this generates will no longer be part of our social action. In the words of John Lennon: "Imagine all the people learning to be free." We are on that path, but we are not there yet.

In my own life, I struggled with fear and other issues. I wanted control over my life. I told Carter I couldn't deal with his games or the challenges of our relationship any more. I begged my angels to keep him away from me. The physical pain it caused me was so intense, though, that I gave up my resolve to exclude him from my life after only one day. Try as I might, I couldn't find a way to go on without him. The alternative to my suffering was to emit unconditional love and that was the course I took. All fear about the relationship ended. I lived the expression "Let go and let God." Suddenly I was free to love unconditionally and that is what felt right for me.

Carter could not help me in this course. He wanted me to understand from the first that the path was going to be lonely at times. He had experienced this all his life. He knew I would have to find this out for myself, to be strong enough and follow the path to enlightenment. All or nothing; no halfway would do.

Unconditional Love

At work, everyone in the house was sick. I had cleaned up so many messes all day and was exhausted. I went to the "garden" to take a break. I settled comfortably in my special chair and felt its beauty surround me. My flagging spirits lifted. Little Girl Self joined me. Carter appeared. I was close to tears, so tired. "I feel the weight of the world on my shoulders," I whined. "How come he knows all about me?" I fussed to my Little Girl Self. "He won't tell me anything about himself." My Little Girl Self stated very plainly, "He is a prince. He has princely secrets." It made perfect sense and I started to laugh. The tears poured from my eyes.

Carter, standing before me, could see I was exhausted. I too was succumbing to the illness I had been fighting all day. Carter reached inside my intestines and gave a quick twist. All my discomfort vanished. He then sent me to bed, wrapping a blanket tightly around me. I asked him to stay. He kissed my cheek, whispering, "You need sleep." The healer in him caressed me and I slept.

As time passed, Carter gradually came closer and I came to depend on his being there. It was hard at first for me to trust him, for he gave me nothing to hang onto. I had had no real trusting relationships as reference points. No one in my life had been trustworthy. I had built walls, putting distance between others and myself. Carter would not tear them down. He wanted me to come to him, on my own. I was a bird on the windowsill, looking in, not leaving the safety of the sill. Carter helped me pack up my past issues in a trunk. We ritualistically sent it and them down the river. I had resisted the urge to remarry. I didn't want to jump from the pot to the fire. I jokingly said I had spent 25 years in marriage, then got a parole for good behavior. I made the statement that any man I would marry would have to be a prince or a pope. Well, Carter fit the bill. I called him my "Pagan Prince."

I invited Carter to watch the sunset with me. He had never done that, he said. It became an evening event. I would sit on the porch or the terraced pool area. Sometimes, Carter would sing to me. "I'm Already There" was our favorite. One evening Carter's son, Adam, joined us. He, too, was able to telepath to me. "Do girls really like this stuff?" he asked. I replied, "Some will, others may be too fearful."

"How come you love my dad? You have never even seen him," Adam asked.

Instead of answering him directly, I told him a story I had once read about King Henry VIII. One of his wives was Anne of Flanders, a Flemish princess. The king had two strong alliances that would enhance his kingdom. These alliances could be secured by taking a wife from either of the other kingdoms. In those days, marriage was about land, money and power. King Henry VIII sent his personal painter to do a portrait of each of the potential wives, for he would choose his wife based on the paintings. The painter set out to do as he was bidden. The first woman was young and silly, pretty but not very bright. The painter was accurate in his portrait, but not inspiring.

The painter then went to the Flemish princess, Anne. She was not a common beauty, but she had an inner radiance. Her life force was captivating. The painter fell in love with this inner light. The portrait he made radiated this essence and his painting was a masterpiece. The king, after seeing it, made his alliance with the Flemish dynasty. Anne of Flanders arrived. She was not what the King had expected at all; Henry was furious and the painter was exiled. King Henry could not send Anne of Flanders back without risking war. So he married her and then sent her to a distant castle. While he formulated how to get rid of her discreetly, King Henry got to know Anne. Gradually, he came to see what the painter had captured in the painting and was impressed with her inner strength and wisdom.

"That inner light is what I see in your father, Adam," I said, "and that means more to me than anything." I could feel the tears in Carter's eyes as I spoke these words.

Carter came to me later that night. It was a beautiful joining.

The words I had said made his love that much stronger. We were so in tune. The unconditional love was so intense, we began to float into space. Up, up, up. Planets, stars, and asteroids all went whizzing by us. I even saw the rings around the Red Planet as we flew. We soared up until the Godhead reached toward us. His countenance was dark and masculine, and he was surrounded by dense clouds. The heavens parted and he looked right at us as he loosed a bolt of lightening that separated us and zapped us back to Earth. What a ride!

The next day, with arms tight around me, Carter asked me, "Shall I leave my space boots by the door?" We giggled like kids. Another day, Carter asked, "How come I keep expecting this love to burn out? It doesn't."

I answered, "I think of our love as a small tree. Each time we come together in love, the tree gets a new ring. The rings make it stronger and stronger. As our history grows, so grows our tree."

"My darling, you're such a romantic," he said.

"That's me, alright. Hope you don't mind. That's how I am. Part of the package."

"I like your package. Don't ever change," he said.

"I don't think that will happen anytime soon," I said.

Despite all of our lovemaking and conversations, there were times that I needed to know Carter was real, that he was not a figment of my imagination. I would beg him to let me feel his heat. Then he would wrap his energy around me and I would light up like a Christmas tree. He is real.

Once, when I was at a Spiritualist meeting, the leader of the group, Reverend Neil, did a ritual to connect us to our spirit guides. Carter took my hand; he was with me. I asked our leader if someone could be with me both in the spiritual and in the physical planes. I couldn't get a consensus. I knew that this being I had talked to on the phone and chatted with online was the same one who held my hand as we called our spirit guides. It was a difficult issue to understand, and for most of my colleagues, it meant uncharted waters.

Carter explained it this way. He had operated on multiple levels all his life, and was able to leave a part of himself with me all the time (as Sam). He could create a morphic field, or telepathic connection, between us. There was an added dimension of empathy and dream sharing. He had the power to create all this. To his surprise, I, too, could create. That was something totally unexpected for him. I had challenged him on a number of occasions during our relationship. He had to study and learn new things. Before we met, he had considered himself "beyond," superior to mere mortals. Carter confided to me that this relationship was something he had never imagined.

"I have talked to you more than any other person in my life, even co-workers," he confessed one evening. "It's taken a long time to open up and really talk with you. I just don't know how. I'm really new at this."

———

I will finish this chapter with an event that occurred in January 2005. I attended an ASD chapter meeting in Danville, Vermont. The presenter was showing "ideograms" that she was able to receive through automatic writing. These messages were from star beings, who, at one point in the presentation, appeared beside her. At least one other attendee and I could see the beings. At the conclusion of the program I went to the presenter and described to her the star beings I had seen:

The first was tall, around six feet, with long white hair and multi-layered robes. I had gotten the sense of a teacher. His tone was soft and compelling, and emanated a masculine aura.

The second being was short, a bit over five feet in height, wearing clothing that reminded me of one I had seen on Tibetan monks during a performance at a local college. It was colorful, and she wore a kind of a lampshade hat with pom-poms dangling from the wide brim that bobbed as she worked. She wore a short top decorated with wonderful designs and colors. Her skirt seemed to stick out stiffly from the lower part of the body. Her aura was definitely female. Oddly enough, the presenter experienced the masculine/feminine energies in just the opposite fashion, which I found quite interesting. My thought is because she could not see them, she felt the loving /nurturing air of the teacher as his feminine side and the energetic, curt persona of the second being as the masculine side. All of this simply reinforced to me the idea of duality in all beings.

The beings followed me home and appeared to me the next night, explaining that they knew of me through my work with the Counsel on the 30th level. They had a project they wanted my help with. They showed me a pair of beings they had created to populate a new planet that had just come into being. The new creatures were lovely. The question put to me was: Should "karma" be instituted on this new planet? I was taken aback, for such a question is monumental and has many facets. I told them that I would need to think about their query for a while. They thanked me for helping them and said they knew I was looking for a motor home to travel to the events that I do. They were going to find a couple that would be what I needed. I thanked them and said it was not necessary to do that. The very next day, I got an e-mail from a local dealer in motor homes, telling me he had just taken in two motor home units he thought I might like to see. How charming is that?

I pondered their question for some time and asked for opinions from several other people. I came up with what I thought was a workable plan, and decided it was time to make my observation. To my surprise, Carter came and took my hand and we went to the Counsel. I told them of my plan: The question of karma should be on hold in the beginning. A re-evaluation might be set for 100 years to assess the pros and cons of the karma issue. The Counsel then asked if Carter and I would be willing to incarnate on this new planet next time around. I'm excited! Is that cool or what?

Chapter 4

Dreams

May 2001:

Carter and I were walking down the concourse of a large building. We were in the middle of New York City. Carter wore his black robe, I had on slacks and a blouse. The hallway was walled in large glass windows. We were 28 stories above ground level. The concrete floor was brightly polished, the stone was gray with flecks of dark and light variance. The sun shone clearly; barely a cloud could be seen in the peaceful blue sky. The city below looked like a miniature from this vantage point. The center of the expansive hall was taken up with raised concrete planters. These planters were full of flora of varying textures and heights. Colored stones formed the contrast to the green of the plants. An Oriental woman in a uniform dress was vacuuming the area.

Suddenly there was a great noise, followed by a flash of light. The whole building shook violently. The Oriental woman screamed "God is coming! God is coming!" She ran to the window and started to open it. I reached her in time to grab her hand and stop her. "Don't open it," I told her. Carter came up to me and placed his hand upon my shoulder. "We must make a leap of faith," he said to me. I stared at him blankly. He repeated, "We must make a leap of faith." This time he took my hand in his. Slowly he opened the window and together, we stepped onto the windowsill. I couldn't look down. The sight of smoke and flames insinuated itself into my mind. I only looked at Carter. Hands clasped, eyes locked, we stepped off the sill. Falling, falling, falling. . .our hands still clasped together, we tumbled through the air. A stream of bright white light appeared. When we intersected the light stream, our fall slowed. We were carried up into the light. When we finally reached our destination, we stood before the Godhead. The Godhead asked us to accept a contract. I will not tell this contract here. It is not appropriate to disclose the contract at this time.

The meaning of this dream was not clear to me until September 11, 2001. On that date, after the attack on the Twin Towers (the World Trade Center), I traveled out of body to "ground zero" and assisted, as did other energy workers, in guiding the lost souls to the stairs of light. I was there, just as in my dream four months before. I did what I could to help. Some souls were not ready to go to the next level. They wandered around dazed. . . unable to let go of this life-time. One uniformed officer brushed off our help. "I still have work still to do," he said. He didn't realize he was no longer in his physical body. I worried about him and checked on him a few days later. He had finally understood and moved on to the next level.

I wondered if I had some obligation to tell of my dream. To whom would I have told this story? Who would have listened or understood? I guess the answer to that is I was able to help the souls who were lost. I was able to make the response quickly because I had been there and knew the way. I could not change their karma, their history. I could only offer guidance to the lost.

June 2001:

I was visiting a parallel dimension where there was a research center. A man in a khaki-colored, short uniform with multiple pockets presided over a drafting board. The barn enclosure that extended past his desk housed some remarkable specimens. The animals were different from any I had ever seen. There was a calf with the head of a large cat (perhaps a cougar) with long whiskers and split ears like a lynx. A duck with long ears occupied one pen. A small horse-goat was contentedly munching grass. I got the idea this was a place where hybrid species were studied. Different species were engineered to develop creatures possessing certain traits that would meet special needs. A golden-skinned young woman was carrying a toddler in a sling. They were both comfortably naked. She seemed to be announcing lunchtime. We all climbed into a Rover. Our destination for the meal was a long, low hacienda. The administrator of the center and his wife graciously provided an excellent repast. The meal featured locally grown and very tasty wine, fruits, and salads of interesting colors and textures. The conversation centered on the station. We discussed its accomplishments and failures.

When the meal was over, we returned to the station research center. The center itself was in an oasis that supported a variety of lovely trees. We passed gardens of flowers and bushes. Herbs and fruit appeared in great abundance. The terrain outside the immediate station was desert and the sand seemed to go on forever.

I saw a huge, brown circus-tent-like structure about fifty feet away. It was three football fields in length; the horizontal view was of peaks and valleys with flags on the peaks— a massive structure to be sure. I astral-traveled to the side of the structure just to estimate its height. I felt very small as I looked to the top, some sixty stories above me.

I returned to the station and, as I turned again to view the huge structure, it burst into flame. We stood transfixed by the enormity of the conflagration. The structure seemed to implode and melt into itself. As it disintegrated, the name of an oil company formed over the front lentil. I watched in horror, thinking all must have perished.

Suddenly and miraculously, people began pouring out from every side. We asked the fleeing occupants how they had escaped. They described a layer of flame-retardant material that had been deployed in every exit from the structure at the first explosion. They were able to make their way out under this layer. The death toll was minimal.

I have some ideas about this dream and its meaning. I thought at first it was about the subsequent 9/11 incident. Maybe the war that resulted was being revealed. My guides tell me the dream was of a plan to save lives. The information was given to me to pass along. I hope that I shared the information with the right people. Edgar Cayce, not a doctor himself, received curatives from his guides. I believe the Universal Consciousness has access to omnipotent information. We all have the ability to tap into that resource—we can become receptors by focusing the universal energy for our collective use.

Another time, I dreamed of cats, five of them, eating from china bowls. The next thing I knew, I was asked to house-sit for a lady with three exotic cats and a daughter with two exotic cats. Yup, you guessed it—their meals were served on china plates and water in china bowls.

A mental motion picture was presented to me: a road with heavy traffic, with cars, trucks, and vans appeared. Everything was moving along smoothly until the van in front of me began to tilt dangerously to the right. Over it went, rolling on its side and the screen went dark.

The next day, I was concerned that I would be involved in an accident. The day went well, nothing occurred, yet I remained cautious. I had a class in Solfeggio tuning forks to attend fifty miles away that evening. Unsure of the location, I started early. I took the old stage road, a less traveled route. I topped a hill and was headed down the other side when I looked to my left and saw a green van rolled onto its right side. I pulled off the road, stopped, and reached the van with my cell phone in hand. Two others drivers had stopped. The van occupants, two little girls and the mother of one of the girls, were helped out and wrapped in blankets. This, I knew, was my dream—I was supposed to be here.

I offered my cell phone. The father was called while the fearful children talked out their mishap. They worked out their concerns and were reassured now that they were safe. My guides had directed me to that spot, at that time, for grace. I was the only other woman on the scene. The young mother confided she had a medical issue that affected her depth perception. Having a nursing background, I had at first feared a drug issue in my initial assessment, but had not shared this thought with anyone. Prescribed or not, the drugs she was on likely contributed to the rollover. Once the authorities arrived, I went on my way to class.

Working nonstop, I fell into bed between shifts. I had tucked a mirror behind the bed to keep it safe. I rolled toward the mirror, and as I closed my eyes, other eyes appeared before me in the mirror. Even though my eyes were closed, I saw gossamer-winged bugs, black and slick, emerge from the viscous part of the eyeball. They were large and shiny, utterly beautiful, as they emerged from the center of the iris. Fascinated, I watched and locked the vision in my brain. I vowed I would paint that scene someday. I guess the moral is if you are working too hard, don't look in the mirror. Since I was not taking any drugs, the vision of those ethereal octopeds wasn't artificially induced.

Dreams take many forms and tell many tales. One of my guides' first assignments for me was to visit a "dream board" on the Internet. There, people would post their dreams and others would offer interpretations. I became a regular and some people would address their inquiries directly to me instead of posting them on the dream board. Working with my guides, I was learning to unravel the content of dreams. This introduction to dream work led to my learning to listen to and work with my guides and ultimately led to mediumship.

One day, while tending a terminal client, I unexpectedly tuned into his brain waves.

A herd of longhorn cattle stampeded headlong up his steep drive. They were red-brown and deeply muscled. The colors were dazzling. Their nostrils flared, sparks flew from their hooves, flecks of sweat dripped from their shiny coats, and steam circled their heads. Dead in the center of their path, a three-year-old little boy stood mesmerized. His hair was dark and all he wore was short white pants (as if a faded photo in black and white.)

I flew down and scooped him into my arms seconds before the herd would have trampled him. We flew up and away until we were over a strange land that I'd never seen before. It was flat with little or no vegetation. Gravelly is how I would describe the soil. It was barren except for strange white pits about 35 feet in diameter. While water collected in the center of the pits, the skeletal remains surrounding the pits suggested that the water must have been toxic. Jagged slabs of white porous rock rimmed the pits, producing a stark outline that pierced the horizon as far as the eye could see. Those pits were spaced perhaps 75 feet apart in all the directions of the compass.

Next we came to a land of trees and rolling hills. There, on the side of a hill, a tractor-trailer was parked. Its side, covered with a blue tarp, was open. Copper-skinned men with jet-black hair were unloading the truck. The foreman was badgering the men and being especially derisive to one man. This man was on his knees before the foreman. The other men paused to watch the harangue. Still carrying the little boy in my arms, I swept down and snatched the hat from the head of the bully. He flailed at me, trying to get his hat back. The kneeling man was able to escape the bully's reach. Everyone else roared with laughter as the bully was forced to contort this way and that grasping for the hat that I held just beyond his grasp. Having escaped, the worker offered a silent prayer of thanks for his release. The bully was totally demoralized by the joke at his expense. His hat seemed to be demonized as it took on a life of its own, dancing away and staying just out of his reach, which also served to unnerve him. I'm sure my presence went undetected.

I believe I had tuned into a life memory of the client I was working with. I have asked around about the landscape of the dream. The only response I received that seems to fit is that gypsum is mined from pits similar to those I described. The client was from western Canada, an area and landscape I have never seen.

The next story is not a dream. It fits well here so I will insert it. I was staying with a family in Stowe, Vermont. I had a nice room with a large bed. The couple that lived there liked to travel, so I house-sat. I cared for their pets and plants. One weekend, the grandchildren and friends came to visit. There were the boy, Sheldon (8) and his friend Adam. They were doing guy things with their grandfather. The girl, Linny, (13) was at loose ends. She followed me around and asked if she could sleep with me in the big bed since she had no friend to keep her company. I agreed that she could stay with me.

I had a computer set up in the room. She played games and chattered until bedtime. My little companion was a very restless sleeper and, since it was a waterbed, her tossing and turning radiated over the whole bed. I finally managed to doze off, only to awaken in the middle of the night about 2 o'clock in the morning. To my astonishment, Linny and three other girls (angels) were sitting cross-legged on the bed talking in a language I didn't know. I just watched and listened. They were all having the best chat, about what, I have no idea.

The Kundalini came to me. I was in bed when the beautiful, coiling, ophidians entwined their lengths up my body. The feel of their sleek scales seeking purchase on my smooth skin sent a series of pleasant shivers up my spine. In one past life, I had been a Mayan and my tribe had worshipped snakes. I admired the coiling muscles of the snakes as they awakened a primal fascination in me. They caressed my body, undulating, pressing, and stirring a sensual response. Understand that this was a most pleasant experience— please don't be repulsed.

Our bodies function like a snake's; peristalsis, it is called. That is how we digest our food and eliminate waste. Watching a snake is like watching our own bodies at work. It has a multifunctional outer skin, beautifully designed to protect from the elements, and predators. Its color and scent glands invite other snakes to play house. The Kundalini awaken that knowledge in us. As you will read in one of my past-life stories, "The Station," we were modified and adapted in "God's image." Snake and reptilian energies reside within each of us. We are a reflection of the energies that are within us. Our physical bodies are evolved vessels that respond to the five senses. Our souls come to Earth to experience the limits of this vessel.

Here are a few ideas that may help you work with your guides in a dream venue. The most common approach...keep a notepad and writing tool beside your bed. Write notes as soon as you come out of a dream; even a few minutes' delay can alter the memory of the dream. I've done dream work workshops and found that key words are useful in interpreting dream messages. Some of those words and concepts include:

A. **Animals**: Dream animals can be your power animals. Horses, wolves, and dogs each have assigned traits that may be part of what you need to learn or help balance your character.

B. **Birds:** Dream birds are all-seeing. Eagles and hawks bring wisdom of far-seeing dimensions. They are able to recognize falsehood in a friend or associate. If they come in a dream, look more closely at issues in your life.

C. **Consequences**: It's time to look at outcomes a second time. Did I do or not do something that had results I did not expect?

D. **The Divine:** You may be searching for a spiritual path. Seeing the Divine suggests that it would be good to reconnect with the Source.

E. **Entrance:** You may be in need of a way into your multi-dimensional self, the seven layers of your consciousness.

F. **Faith**: You may need to develop a deeper trust in yourself, your guides, or in some of the other people in your life.

G. **Greed**: You may feel unfulfilled, hungry for more money, love, and material things, or even divine inspiration.

H. **Happiness**: You create your own happiness. No one else can give it to you. It springs from your own center of authority.

I. **Identity**: You are who you are. Your plan for this life is different from every other person's and your idea of abundance may be very different. That is OK; you are OK!

J. **Joy**: Pure joy is an inner emotion. It stimulates release of endorphins in the brain that flow to your furthest extremities.

K. **Karma**: These are the lessons you agreed to learn in this lifetime. Step back and reflect; there is no judgment of good or bad, just lessons.

L. **Love**: Unconditional love is not a tool to be given or withheld for a price, but instead, constant, unwavering support.

M. **Meditation**: Time to pause and allow the body to enter an altered state that cleanses the spirit and connects with the universe.

N. **Nature:** Hug a tree. Listen to the sound of the birds, pat a dog, and lift your eyes to a sunset. The Earth is our planet, a living, breathing entity.

O. **Open**: Be open to the help and love around you. The universe wants to encourage your joy and happiness.

P. **Prayer**: The Akashic Records hold all your prayers. Brain waves change when prayer is invoked and it can be more powerful than drugs.

Q. **Quest**: Your quest is the shamanic journeywork that may unite you with your power animals, bring you to an altered state, and/or open your consciousness to the Universe.

R. **Response**: You're reaching out to accept the energy of the universe and help with the cleansing of Mother Earth.

S. **Sort**: Peel away the layers of information to find the truth that resonates for you. Your path is different from every other path.

T. **Talent:** You are a gifted being. Others can learn from you. Your role is significant to the universal plan.

U. **Understanding**: Wars result when understanding is misplaced. We each have a unique point of view. Understanding is the umbrella.

V. **Vision**: You search and find joy and beauty; a world at peace is visionary. Visualizing it is the first step to creating it.

W. **Will**: This is a free-will zone. We can make our own choices that affect our future. We must accept the results of those choices.

X. **X-ray**: Look at the deeper levels of the issue for the meaning…a fish may either refer to a fishing trip or mean a fish out of water.

Y. **You:** are a special person, unique, needed.

Z. **Zen**: Live in the now. The past cannot be changed, only recorded. The future is yet to be written, so our daily actions create our future.

The above list provides a starting point for a personal jargon to be established between you and your guides. Once established, you can use it to work out the meaning of your dreams. If you ask your guides to use your code, it is one way they can communicate with you through your dreams. Understand, though, that you have to ask in order to get an answer! At night, before going to sleep, ask for a dream that will help you solve a particular issue, clarify a course of action, or any number of things. Writing the question on paper can not only clarify it in your mind, but also be the start of your dream log. Please be sure to ask that you remember the dream on waking!

My dream code involves black animals. If, while I'm dreaming, I see a rather vicious black dog, I can be sure that I will meet an authority figure and am not going to enjoy the meeting. Example: being stopped by a police officer in a black uniform. A dream of little black squirrels and chipmunks, tumbling all over each other, translated into some Jamaicans that I worked with for six months.

In one dream, a black wolf appeared along with a white wolf. I was standing behind a tree. A young child giggled and ran behind me. I was too far from the house and the wolves were crossing the path between the tree and house. Suddenly, I saw someone fall and could not tell who it was. The scene disappeared as if a curtain had literally dropped in front of my eyes. The next day, as I was getting water at a spring, I was climbing the seven cement steps I had climbed countless times before with two gallon jugs full of water in my hands. The next thing I knew, I was tumbling backward down the cement steps. I landed in a heap at the bottom. I was so well wrapped in winter clothes, I managed to get away with a scrapped knee and elbow. This translated to the black wolf representing the fall and the white wolf representing minimal injury. That worked for me!

Whenever I see black animals in my dreams, I am alert to potential issues that bode ill for me. You may well develop such a connection with your guides. If such a pattern repeats in your dreams, take heed…a message is being given to you. "Forewarned is forearmed." That doesn't mean you can completely change the outcome. However, you may be able to defuse the situation. I couldn't stop the fall (I have benign vertigo) but the heavy clothes protected me, diminishing the effect of the fall.

If you are plagued by nightmares, I offer some possible solutions. In dreams, you are actually in control. In the clutch of a nightmare, you may manifest a weapon to slay your adversary or pull out of the distressing scene and enter a summer day with singing birds. It is your mind that permits you to come from the place of authority and create your dream. An effective tool for preventing or minimizing nightmares is to meditate immediately before sleep, thereby clearing non-beneficial thoughts from your mind, with intent! Think pleasant, calm, and joyous thoughts or of such places before sleep. The mind cannot discern the difference between an actual event and the picture of an event. For instance, the television version of war appears to the brain just as if you were actually in that war. The body produces adrenalin, a very strong drug. If you try to sleep after such an event, your body is still dealing with the "fight or flight" response. It doesn't take a brilliant mind to envision nightmares after this kind of stimulus.

Try to make the thoughts you fall asleep with be your most calming ones. Sleep time is the opportunity for detoxifying the body, both physically and mentally. To make the most of that opportunity, you may find it best to prepare a ritual designed to create that result. Be it meditation, relaxation tapes, happy thoughts, or whatever else works for you, remember to make the most of the opportunity.

Happy dreaming!

Chapter 5

Reincarnation

I have been given a gift, the gift of understanding. I share that understanding wherever I can and offer the understanding to any who wish to step outside the box and accept that our limits are only our ego-based, self-imposed walls. Reality is as limitless or as restricted as we souls choose it to be. Each of us is the sum of multidimensions. We create our own future. Clients ask me the future; I can give them possible futures, but only they can make it happen. We are the artists of our own futures. The canvas before us is blank; we add the color and the story. It is our free will that paints the picture of our life.

I was doing readings at a small bookstore in Stowe, Vermont. One day, a woman wandered in; she had a lost look. I asked if I could help her. We connected immediately. Anna, the woman, told how the spirits of the dead had tormented her for years. She had been treated for mental illness (Western medicine's way of dealing with the issue), was disabled from work, and was unable to sleep. I reached out to her and gave her a hug.

"Dear one," I told her, "you are not ill. You have a gift. The world has need of you. Come to American Society of Dowsers in Danville. Surround yourself with people who can appreciate your gifts and validate your experiences and help you develop your ability in a positive way." I then asked if she could see my angel and guides with me.

Anna replied, "Yes. I think the one on your left is your son." I was awestruck! Tears of joy filled my eyes.

Boye was my fourth child. On the 6th of August in 1969, about midnight, I told my husband, "The baby is coming." He answered, "I'll call my mother," thinking that she would stay with the children while we went to hospital. "Too late," I said. "The babe is coming now." He said, "I'll call the doctor." There was an old-town doctor six miles away. I prepared for the event and asked my husband to bring some things into the bedroom: towels, a shoelace, and a small blanket. Minutes later, I directed him to gently turn the baby's head as he appeared between my legs. The baby boy slipped into his waiting hands. I told him to hold the baby on one arm and clear the mouth of mucus. The little boy had poor color. I showed my husband how to do CPR. I encouraged him, saying "You're doing everything right. Don't worry. He will not live but you have done all you can. He is in God's hands."

I showed my husband how to wrap the shoelace around the umbilical cord in two places and then cut between the ties. I was busy delivering the afterbirth when the doctor arrived. He asked my husband if I knew what was happening. My husband replied, "She knows." The doctor, a Catholic, asked for a bowl of water. He baptized the little boy "Boye" with water as the flame of life left the tiny body cradled in his father's arms. I was ordered to stay in bed. My husband was directed by the doctor to take the body to the morgue.

It wasn't until much later I learned that two of our close friends had heard on the radio scanner that the doctor had been summoned. It had been my wish that Boye's life, though short, might help other babies to live, so we offered his body to the University of Vermont Medical School. Our friends waited outside our house and they were the ones who drove my husband and son to the university to deliver the tiny body to the medical school morgue.

Finally, in 1991, I learned that aspirin had caused Boye's death. I was talking to a research doctor who had worked on aspirin and knew its effects on a fetus. The damage had been done before I knew life was growing inside me. The aspirin had attacked the major organs as they formed in the tiny cytoplast that would grow into the tiny babe who briefly flared to life and was as quickly gone.

It was Boye whom I met in Spirit/Faerie. He had waited 31 years to tell me I was forgiven for taking the aspirin that had resulted in his death. Later, I went back to see him and found he was not there; he had moved on to the next step in his soul life.

That day in the store, Anna told me what that next step was: Boye was one of my angel/guides now. I had known that one of my guides was a little one, for I perceived him to be about two feet long. When my angel/guides came to clean my body as angels will do when asked, he had jumped in with such enthusiasm (like a kid doing a cannonball into water), it had taken my breath away. "Take it easy," I had chided. I asked that he be a little bit gentler with me. He learned to be much calmer with his work over time.

I like to listen to books on tape. One night, as Boye was making his visit, a scary part came on the tape. Boye was just inches above my chest. I heard him let out a gasp and felt his energy tickle my torso in a jump of surprise. His eyelashes brushed my cheek.

Another time, I went to see the movie *Lord of the Rings: The Two Towers*. Boye sat on my left shoulder. I could feel just the slightest pressure there, and every once in a while, he would brush my hair ever so slightly. When the movie got really scary, he would hide behind my head and take in a surprised breath. I had to giggle; it felt so strange having this little spirit on my shoulder gasping and hiding behind my head.

It wasn't until Anna mentioned my son on my left side that I understood this little angel was my Boye, the babe I had given to God so long ago. I had begged forgiveness from him in Spirit/Faerie and now he was with me as one of my angel/guides. How wondrous is that?!

I knew I was too close to the question. At the next ASD chapter meeting, I asked my dear friend Dan Churchill if my understanding was correct about Boye. "YES! YES! YES!" was the message he got from his guides. How amazing and wonderful life really is. Most of us only touch the surface of reality.

I had gained understanding with these revelations. I asked my angel/guides what realm Boye was working from? They told me that he was in the realm of Archangel Raphael, the healing realm. The reader may remember that I am from the realm of Archangel Michael, the loving realm. Boye is a private in the army of healing angels. He is working as one of my medical angels. As he progresses in his understanding in the medical/healing venue, he has chosen to work with others and me to learn to heal the physical body.

One day, when he has reached the level of knowledge necessary to pass the requirements, he will choose his parents and his time of birth will be set. He will then reincarnate on earth and eventually become a doctor/healer. That is the angel way. For the time being, however, he is with me, learning all he can from my health needs. My joy is boundless.

It's All Connected

Tara, my dog, a beloved Rottweiler and the companion of my life, died. It was fall and I buried her in the woods bright with colored leaves. Two weeks later, Tara came to me. I saw the dirt on her back where I had covered her body. So glad to see me, she was wiggling all over and grinning from ear to ear. She bounced down on her front paws. "Happy dog, happy dog," she crooned. She had two little boys with her; they were about two and three years old. They had blue snowsuits on, red mittens on their hands and black boots on their feet. I was very sure I did not know them. Tara, my dear dog, was showing me her new job as a psychopomp.

A psychopomp is a guide that leads souls that are crossing over to the 25th level. That level is also known as "purgatory," "recovery," and the "planetary logos." It is the first stop after the soul leaves the body. I thanked Tara for bringing the children to me and told her that it was now time for her to take the little boys to their destination. I patted her head and pointed the way. I was so happy for her. She had always loved children. This seemed to be a perfect role for her.

While she was alive, Tara had tried to sing. She did not howl as dogs do, but attempted to change chords as much as her dog's vocal cords would allow. Every morning, when the National Anthem came on, Tara would sing along. I had asked my guides if she had been a singer in a past life. Yes, was the answer. She had been a singer and also had been very cruel to animals. For that reason, she needed to come back to spend a life as a dog. Tara had to learn the lesson from the other side to feel what it was like to be an animal. That is how karma works.

I have heard many people voice the opinion that animals have no soul. That is totally incorrect. I have met many animal souls in Spirit/Faerie. When I do readings, very often a beloved pet will come through.

The day after Tara brought the little boys to see me, I was substitute teaching for an 8th grade class. One of the children knew I was a medium. In one of the classes, a young man asked if I could find his brothers. The story came out that his two brothers had been killed in a car accident with their grandmother before he was born. The brothers had been 11 and 12 when they had been killed. The boy was 13, so by our time, that would have made the brothers about 24 and 25. I told him I would look into it for him.

I posted the question on www.AstralSociety.com. I related the story of my dog bringing the two little boys to me. I described the clothes they wore and their ages. One of the regular contributors to the site, Peace2U, had just moved to Alaska. She read my post and replied that two little boys of that age had drowned in a nearby river. What really freaked her was the clothes they had been wearing were exactly as I had described. Well! This I needed to confirm. Then my guides put the idea in my head that these two boys were the brothers I had been asked to locate. Could this be true?

At the next meeting of ASD, I told Dan the story about my dog and the two boys, adding the information about the drowning in Alaska and my young 8th-grader asking about his siblings. Could it be all tied together? The response was a resounding "Yes!"

The little boys, the brothers, had died in a car accident in 1988. Something about their death had to be rerun or retried so they reincarnated in 1998 and 1999 to experience the death again. This time, they died by drowning in 2001. That was the only lesson they had to retake before they could move on. Truth is stranger than fiction. By inserting me into this drama, my angel/guides were teaching me about reincarnation. The little boys had to die for their lesson. I had to observe for my lesson.

Roger

I was camping by the river. I had a borrowed tent; there were still pieces missing after I had done my best to put it together. The tent hung about a foot and a half off the ground. Oh, well! I went around breaking down the tent poles until the tent was at ground level. I was tired and achy, for I had started my day at about 7 that morning. It was now 8 o'clock in the evening and I still didn't have a bed. I was here for the ASD convention, it was early June and the nights were still cold in the Northeast Kingdom, as my part of the world is called.

The convention would run for a week and had started this day. There had been so much to see and do that I had been on my feet all day. There I was setting up my little cubby, my cot (a chaise lounge) with an air mattress covered by a wool blanket and my polar sleeping bag. Everything looked so toasty, toasty. But I was not ready to go to bed yet. I set up the chair, the water jug, the portable toilet, and a box of wet wipes. I never use a flashlight, though I suppose I should. I washed up and brushed my teeth. At last, I could strip down and snuggle into that sleeping bag. I glanced toward the chair to my left. There sat my brother Roger.

You may recall that on my first trip to Spirit/Faerie, it was my brother Roger who had asked me to give a message to his wife. He had died in a car accident in 1989. Well, whatever! He was sitting right there in my tent, on my chair, on the bank of the river. I was so surprised to see him, all I could say was "Hi!" He said he would stay and keep me company. I was so tired I just thanked him and promptly fell asleep. Although I had visited him in Spirit/Faerie a few times, this was the first time he had come to me.

The next morning, I awoke but stayed snuggled in my cozy, warm sleeping bag. My cold nose told me that "warm" was not a good adjective for the day. I remembered my brother but he was no longer sitting where I had left him. I chided myself for not asking him about his visit.

That afternoon, I attended a workshop with John Kelly, entitled "A Shamanic Journey." (John's contact information is in the "Resource" section of this book). John uses a Native American drum to enhance a guided meditation. During the workshop, I began my quest and almost immediately, I met a large eagle. He scooped me into his beak and carried me to the top of a tall mountain somewhere out West; I saw sandstone mountains and cactus-covered plains. The bird dropped me into a nest high at the top of a cliff. I plummeted down through the nest, falling deep in the center of the mountain. Then I rolled out of a cave opening at the bottom of the mountain. A large brown bear (my power animal) came galloping up to me. He tossed me onto his back and off we went at great speed. He took me into the mountains to a pow-wow site with a large gathering of Native Americans. At the gathering, I learned the purpose of my visit but cannot reveal more about the journey here.

I finished my quest early so I decided to pop over to Spirit/Faerie to connect up with my brother, Roger. I wanted to discover the reason for his visiting me the night before. I found him and he told me he had come to me because I could recognize him and he would know that his first attempt to come to this side of the veil had been successful. I replied, "Now that you know the way, will you go to be an angel/guide to one of your grandchildren?" His answer was "No, I will be an angel/guide for your grandson, Alex." I was stunned, and then I understood.

Roger had been an athlete, a bodybuilder, and a professional football player. When we were kids, my sister and I would go with him to the cemetery in his convertible car. He would push the car while we steered it around the paved paths, about a half-mile or more each trip. He did this to build his muscles. I have no idea how much the car weighed, but I remember it being a full-sized, 1950s muscle car.

My grandson Alex was born with achondroplasia, or dwarfism. He will spend this lifetime with a physical limitation. The glitch on his chromosome string will keep him from attaining the athletic excellence of his great-uncle Roger. In his role as angel/guide to Alex, Roger will learn how to cope with physical limitation. As he watches over Alex (helping when asked, as is the angel way), Roger, too, will be learning a lesson. Assisting Alex will give him insight into the other side of the lesson of living with a physical limitation. Once Roger learns the lessons, he will make his choice to incarnate in his next lifetime, not as the athlete of his most recent lifetime, but as a person with physical limitations.

The Essence of Reincarnation

Do you understand the concept of reincarnation better now? I have given you some detailed examples of how the system works. The soul is a basic energy-charged unit. It begins its growth at a low vibration, compatible with that of Mother Earth. The unit (soul) takes on a vessel (body). This body is one that will be appropriate for the lessons agreed upon for this lifetime. Each time the soul unit learns the lessons agreed to, it takes on a higher vibration. This higher vibration is charted as a soul-growth level.

The chart starts at the "infant soul," neophyte, or freshman level. This is the soul level at which a new soul to Earth vibrates. This is a very difficult level. The soul has come from a oneness, the source of all energy. It is dropped, alone, into a very scary world. The soul feels orphaned in a strange and foreign land, for it has come from total love and light. There are no rules or maps to guide the soul, and it is so very lonely. From total inclusion to total exclusion. The soul has free will, as well as two guides/ angels, who have come to be with the soul. They may only help the soul if asked because of the soul's free will.

The soul we are following has learned the lessons agreed upon for its first incarnation. The transformation to discarnate (death) has occurred. A review takes place. Lessons are examined. Its vibration level has increased. The soul will now rest and decide the next lessons it will learn.

It is my understanding that no new souls will be incarnating on Mother Earth again. The school is closed, so to speak. That doesn't mean that the birth rate will go down, but simply that no more neophytes will enter the system. Any new lifetimes will be filled with souls already in the system.

It is the plan for mankind to evolve to the next dimensional level. You may have heard of this. Man is a third-dimensional being at present. It is the God plan that we shall become fourth— and even fifth-dimensional beings. There will be some physiological changes to accommodate this higher vibration. Many of us now present are here for the change. We are awaiting "the hundredth monkey," the phenomenon that happens to a species once critical mass has been reached.

The new being to emerge will no longer have the "fight or flight" response that has ruled our solar plexus since our emergence on this planet. We will no longer respond to perceived fear by flooding our bodies with adrenalin, a substance that eats away at the linings of our organs. We will not run away or stand and fight. That need will be gone.

The new being will answer in love and light, once the understanding is reached that what we call "death" is just a change and not an end at all. It is the graduation from one lifetime of lessons to an opportunity to move on and try new experiences.

Soul Levels

The life of a single soul may encompass a thousand lifetimes on Earth and in other planetary systems. I have reached 563 lifetimes on earth and 413 in other planetary systems. In so doing, I have reached the transcendental, freshman level, where I vibrate at approximately 18 gigahertz. This is the vibration level that makes it possible for me to connect to the other levels in mediumship.

One time, I took a trip to David Stanger's place for an event. As I passed through his standing stones, a portal opened up for me and I was transported to another level, the 30th level. When I returned from this adventure, I was vibrating at 23 gigahertz and as it turned out, I had jumped to a transcendental senior level. I had been shifted off-balance in my aura and it took six months to realign myself. These challenges are some of the issues that will have to be dealt with before mankind can make the shift to the next dimension.

To help you understand better: the soul levels are infant, baby, young, mature, old, transcendental, and infinite. Each soul level has four "grades" associated with it: freshman, sophomore, junior, and senior, as follows.

Infant soul	freshman	sophomore	junior	senior
Baby soul	freshman	sophomore	junior	senior
Young soul	freshman	sophomore	junior	senior
Mature soul	freshman	sophomore	junior	senior
Old soul	freshman	sophomore	junior	senior
Transc. soul	freshman	sophomore	junior	senior
Infinite soul				

This may sound a lot like school to you. You would be absolutely correct. The purpose of these soul levels and the lifetimes involved to ultimately reach the higher vibration of an infinite soul is to learn. We reincarnate to learn lessons from both the dark and the light. "Karma" is the Eastern term used for these lessons.

As the single soul learns the karmic lessons for each lifetime, that knowledge creates a higher vibration. An infant soul vibrates very close to Mother Earth's own vibration, whereas the infinite soul vibrates near that of the Godhead. The infinite soul level can appear on earth, but resides in the higher realms. Jesus, Mohammad, and Buddha are all infinite souls. So it goes, incarnate or discarnate, each soul is working toward vibrating with the Source, or Godhead.

Soul Mates

To help clarify things more completely for you, let me include a piece here about soul mates. I have heard and read a lot of misinformation about this issue. Once a soul decides what karmic lessons will be studied in the upcoming lifetime, a family or group is gathered together to work with the soul to learn the lesson. This group is known as the "soul group." Each member of the group also has lessons to learn. Some of the lessons will be light, where as others will be dark. An example of such a "light-dark" lesson would be when one of the soul group agrees to be a murderer, while another comes in as the victim. Each member of the group is a soul mate to every other member of the group. The chosen lessons of the group change as the lessons are learned.

To use a personal example, my son Boye is now a medical angel. Another of our soul family, my brother Roger, is now an angel/guide for my grandson Alex.

Your mother is your soul mate, your father is your soul mate. A soul mate is any of the group who has incarnated with you to help you learn your karmic lessons. Depending on the karmic issues, meeting your soul mate may or may not be pleasant. Karma seems to last a whole lifetime. Soul mates come and go, depending on their roles in your karma. The soul mate who helped you learn your lessons has fulfilled its role. You no longer have anything in common. It is at this time you may seek a life partner, with new karmic issues between you and that person. You now have the opportunity to face new challenges. You may decide to get in some "extra credit" classes. The normal course of events is that if you incarnate as an "old soul freshman" level, you will leave this lifetime at an "old soul sophomore" level. However, since we are here as transitional beings involved in the change from third-dimensional to fourth-dimensional beings, we may be given the opportunity to add lessons to our soul and raise our vibration levels.

In my case, I have gone from "old soul" to "transcendental soul" in a very short span—in this lifetime. You may recall that in his foreword to this book, Dan Churchill mentioned that I was the only person he had ever read who ranked 100 on the karma chart. I replied that it only meant that I'm the valedictorian for this class. It was a joke at the time, though I think it did indicate that I have begun new lessons to make me compatible with my twin flame.

Twin Flames

To better illustrate for you the process of incarnation, five of my own 129 lifetimes spent with my twin flame, Carter, are shared with you in the later chapters of this book. We have evolved from the same soul over those lifetimes together. Twin flames are part of the same soul that has splintered. We have helped one another learn lessons and experience lifetimes on Earth and other planets. These lifetimes have been known to me since I was eight years old, when they were presented as lucid dreams. I asked to remember my past lives. It was not until I connected to my angel/guides that I learned the meaning of these dreams I had experienced for years.

Carter and I agreed to meet again in this lifetime. I have a lot of work to do in order for us to be soul equals. We seem to be climbing up the hill from opposite sides. Our goal is to meet at the top and form a united flame. We have met the feminine aspect of the Source, or Godhead. Carter and I were opening our chakras to one another, with a wonderful rainbow of colors rising between us. I asked the angels to raise our vibrations. As they surrounded us with their energy, we floated higher and higher into other dimensions until, at last, we were surrounded by the ultimate energy of the Source. In another story I relate in this book, the Male Source energy zapped us with a bolt of lightening. This time, the Female Source cradled us in love and light. Words fail to convey the feeling of oneness we felt with the Source.

I will give a very personal statement here: It is my belief that when Carter and I meet in physical form in this lifetime, we will be the "hundredth monkey," and that the spiritual critical mass for the planet will be reached. The new dimension will emerge at this event.

Chapter 6

Animals

When I moved to the country, I acquired a large house and lots of critters. I never went looking for the animals; they just appeared on my doorstep, a few at a time. I had a big barn, lots of grass—why not? There was nothing I enjoyed more than watching them interact with one another. I have a great respect for all beasts and nature in general. Often, the ways of mankind seem somehow ridiculous.

Native American shamans and healers the world over take on the form of animals, birds, and even amphibians, in their journey work. I told you earlier about my shape-shifting experience as a lioness. Later, you will read about my past life as a lion, which exists in the stored memory of my soul; I can call it to the surface at will. Tribal totems of the Native Americans seek to inspire members of the clan with the strengths of their totem animals. The goal of a quest is often to receive wisdom from the tribe's and individual's power animals. As I shared in an earlier chapter, my quest to find my power animals put me in touch first with a bear, then a snake, and finally the hawk.

Animals in my Life

The horses were lifelong friends. Nilla was my chestnut mare; I had delivered her in 1981. She came out in a sac, which I tore open. Her little eyelashes fluttered. She wiggled and squirmed out of the sac. There she stood on four wobbly legs. A circle of children watched. Nilla wobbled up to each child, looked interested, then moved on. After completing the circle, she found her mother and located the teats and began to suck. Amazing!

Daimler, a standardbred gelding, was retrained after seven years at Saratoga and came from the farm where my children took lessons. He was tall, 17 hands at the withers. I got a buggy and drove for miles. All the children and grandchildren who fit sat on the seat. The rest straddled the horses, still more joined with bicycles, sometimes even the dogs and cats joined the entourage. Once a sheep got loose and followed along. Daimler made it clear that he was insulted, sidling and sidestepping and sighing. Playing crossing guard to that damn sheep was decidedly beneath his dignity. The horses endured showers, tail braids, parades, performance jitters, eventing, trailering, and being ridden by experienced and novice riders.

One autumn, I told my oldest daughter, Tamar, there was a view she just had to see. I took my oldest grandson, Beau, up on Daimler. Tamar, pregnant, had Keenan, another one of my grandsons, on Nilla. We took a rocky path to the top of a ridge. There before us lay an astounding view of the town, the church steeple, the lake, and the mountains beyond. Everything was decked out in fall colors. God, it was beautiful! Made you glad to be alive. Those horses knew they carried precious cargo. They picked their way over the rocks with ballet-dancer grace. With more experienced riders, they could have barrel-raced with wild abandon.

I so well remember another time I took a ride on Daimler on a late September afternoon. It was so beautiful, I just wanted to ride on forever. Warm rain came down and then the hot sun would appear and dry up the rain. I knew I had to go back to work from 11 that evening to 7 the next morning, so I decided to take a "short cut." You know the kind. It was a trail I had been on years before. Well, I got into this field, couldn't find away out, couldn't find the way in. It was getting dark. Round and round this field we went. Finally, I threw up the reins, saying right out loud, "I give up." Daimler took his cue. Straight as an arrow, he picked his way back to the road. Once back on track, I started to turn him. No dice! He was headed home and no one, nothing, was going to get him lost again.

In the winter, we would attach long leather lines to the box sled. The brave would put on skis. Holding the lines, they would be dragged along behind the sled. (In Norway, they call it *ski-joerring*.) Even though the corners of the trails were banked, people would often fly off into the air over the snow banks. The horses had as much fun as the children. At night, the full moon would gleam on the snow, providing a perfect backdrop to the fun and games. We'd head inside for hot cocoa and a warm fire. The horses, under warm blankets as they cooled down, had their treats too.

To be sure, the animals saved my sanity. Each morning, they would greet me with heads extended. In whatever language they used, the cacophony of the barn was blissful and welcoming. Once fed, they peacefully enjoyed their portions. I would sit on a bale of hay, inhaling the aroma of steam from their backs, mixed with hay and grain. A great feeling of peace on earth and good-will pervaded the entire scene. I often think I was born 100 years too late. When I was young, I loved to hear my Nana tell of driving the horse and buggy. One day, they encountered a motor car on the road. The horses sat right down in the middle of the road and wouldn't move until that infernal machine cleared out. Secretly, I dreamed of going cross-country in a horse and wagon. That had only happened in a past-life. Nevertheless, I did my share of carriage driving. Mile after glorious mile, sometimes at a stately walk, other times at a crisp trot, and, very occasionally, a flat-out race. I would sing to the tattoo of the hoofs on the road.

You can experience a whole different world from the buggy, things missed when you whiz by in a car.

One night, driving back from a 4th of July party, I came around a bend in the road. There before me, I beheld the most strikingly beautiful sight. A miniature metropolis, a fairyland, a meadow full of fireflies blinking in the night. It was so breathtaking, I had to stop and watch the spectacle. I was privy to a magical event. I half-expected little beings to come and spirit me away, Gulliveresque, as they had in *Gulliver's Travels*. It was hard to break the spell. The thunder of fireworks boomed in the distance. Reality intruded. With a flip of the reins, I was on my way. Yet the magic lingered. The night took on a surreal dimension, the darkness cut by the buggy lamps. The sky was awash in flashes of color, the booms enhanced by the tattoo of the horses' hooves. Could anyone witness such a vision and not be inspired? I continued the two miles homeward, and every time I passed that spot, the memory would jump to consciousness. I would always look to see if maybe one dear little fairy would peek out at me. "I...there be magik in this place."

My cat, Jerry, was a beautiful dark tabby with silky-soft fur. One day, he disappeared into the woods and I mourned his absence. Some time later, as I lay sleeping with my arm extended off the bed, I felt his soft fur rub against my hand. This was something he had always done. Then I felt his little paws scampering up the bedclothes. He came to visit me several times after he had passed.

It was a week before Christmas, about midnight, that Daimler died. I was connected to Carter and suddenly saw a test pattern in my head. My head began to throb and I thought I was going to vomit. I instantly went out of body and began to float above the stable where Daimler was. There, I saw him lying on the dirt. Then I returned to my physical body. I awoke at five the next morning and Daimler appeared to me. He was young and beautiful. He pranced around, his tail flagging, his coat shiny. I was so happy to see him. He was thirty years old when he passed; we had been together for twenty. I felt it a privilege to have spent so many wonderful hours together. We had shared buggy and sleigh rides, saddle rides, and now, he allowed me to share his passing. The young Daimler wore a rope headstall and stood quivering as I reached up and unhooked the rope. "There you are, dear friend," I said in a calm, loving voice. "No more fences, no more hard winters. Fly over the rainbow bridge and be free." With that, he turned and I pointed the way heavenward. I watched him gallop away into the distance, sparkling light streaking behind, toward the rainbow bridge. I wept for joy. I know my guides have given me a great gift by allowing me to experience such events. I am humbled to this day with the honor.

Later that day, I decided to honor my dear friend Daimler with a ceremony. I borrowed a CD of Native American drumming from Jack. I set up a sacred place with Daimler's bridle and saddle, a picture of him, and arranged candles, incense, and some crystals. When everything was ready, I lit the candles and started the drums. As soon as the first drumbeats filled the room, I was transported to an Indian village. There I found a campfire and many braves dancing around as the sparks from the fire flew high into the sky. Beyond the circle of firelight, there were tepees. Women and children sat and watched the fire and the dancers. Slowly, my room reappeared and I resumed the ritual of honor for my friend. I gave honor to the Universe and Mother Earth, the cardinal points, and the elementals. I gave thanks for the opportunity to have shared the life of my dear friend, Daimler. I wished him a safe journey and great happiness. To this day, Daimler will come in spirit and put his great head on my shoulder, bringing me messages from the spirit world. Other mediums and spiritualists have given me word of him as well.

There was a doggy camp the first week in September at the Mountaineer Motel that I go to do my "executive workout," consisting of a swim, sauna and hot tub session. As I stepped into the hot tub on this particular day, I was bombarded with telepathic info-bytes from the dogs. One complained his owner had changed his food and it was giving him a stomach ache. Another had a sore hip from traveling. I could not tell which dog had which complaint. The thoughts just emanated from the animals and because I am receptive, I could hear their thoughts. I had to shut down the input; it wasn't my ears that were receiving the information, but my brain. I had to ask my guides to protect me from all the stimuli.

My Work with Animals

Animals, on the whole, are much more psychic than humans. They use the ability in their natural state to communicate. Because of my highly tuned receptivity, it is not surprising then that I should "hear" them. For years, I have been helping pet owners understand their pets as part of my work.

All of us have had, or will have, lifetimes as animals as part of our soul learning. That animals have souls is understood. I find evidence of it all the time in the readings I do. Dogs and cats, horses and birds, will come through from the other dimension. If they have not developed the ability to project clearly, I see them as furry little balls. When I focus with intent, I can usually get a clear picture of the spiritual animal that wishes to give a message during a reading.

Archangel Zadechiel, who rules the lower 14th level where the animals reside, gave me this assignment. He came to me in a dream. There were many riders on all sizes and shapes of animals. In the dream, they were galloping headlong around a rocky out-crop. Some of the riders wore Arabian headgear and robes. One such rider, mounted on a very fast, small, light-colored horse, turned to me as I sat under a tall cactus plant. He said, "Ask her if she wants to ride," and dashed away. There appeared before me a tall figure wrapped in a blue robe. When I say tall, I mean *TALL*. I could not estimate his height so I traveled to his shoulder and looked down to the spot under the cactus plant where I had been sitting. It looked like a long way down. I have heard others refer to him as forty feet tall, though I have since dowsed and have got-ten thirty feet. His robe covered all but a small oval of his face. He asked me if I would like to work with animals. I, of course, said yes. The being said he would allow me to psychically con-nect to animals and that he would teach me to work with them. I thanked him and we parted.

Readings I do often feature dogs and cats, who are now in the spirit realms waiting to send love and light to their former part-ners. One of the most spectacular pet visions I ever had was at the Spiritualist Convention a number of years ago. I was doing a gal-lery reading when I came to the sixth person. The moment I con-nected to her vibration, a stunning bird flew before my eyes. It seemed to be rising from the flames like some fabled phoenix. It had the colorful plumes of an exotic parrot, but was smaller. It totally blew me away, as most of my readings are in black and white. I told the lady what I was seeing. She knew immediately that her dear bird, a pet that had died in a fire, had reached out to her from the other dimension. She was overwhelmed with the message of love the beautiful bird sent to her. I was awed by the beautiful colors of the picture I had received.

I once had a funny experience with the spirit of a cat. I was doing a reading for a teenage girl, whose mother had given her a gift certificate for a reading. I was describing a little dog that was coming to her. He looked like one of those RCA Victorola record dogs, with a patch over one eye, cropped ears, and a couple of other dark patches along his body. She said she had never had a dog, only a cat. I said, "Well, this is no cat." I asked my guides if this was her dog. The answer came back that it was indeed her cat. The little beast had been raised with dogs originally and had adopted the persona of a dog. Go figure! Since that reading, I have run into other cat owners who swear their cats think they are dogs. Who am I to disagree?

Dogs are often used as pyschopomps. I have already told of my dog Tara and how she brought two little boys to me after her death. A client of mine asked me about her son, who had been killed in a car "accident." (I hesitate to use the word "accident," as there is really no such thing.) Though I tried, I was unable to locate him immediately. Further search indicated that he was not aware of his death. When I asked if I should find him and help him to make the trip, I was told that his dog had been sent to perform this task. I then asked the client if her son had a dog. She replied in the affirmative. I then explained that the dog had been sent as a pyschopomp. Once the son had moved to the next level,

I was able to reach him after about six weeks in recovery, the first stop after the soul transitions out of the physical body we refer to as death.

One of my "jobs" here is also to interpret dreams. Many dreams involve animals. I usually offer the Native American wisdom of the animals as messengers. If an animal appears to you in a dream, or even unexpectedly in the physical, try to imagine the attributes of the animal. These may provide you with insights into what message you are being offered. The hawk may represent foresight. The sighting of a hawk in a dream or in the physical may bring the message that you may want to look at a situation from a different angle. The bear may indicate protection. A wolf is known to be very family oriented, for wolves protect their young at all cost, and are powerful and quiet, capable of seeing without being seen.

Even the earliest man carved animals on the walls of caves. We humans have also had a deep connection to animals during much of history. The Native Americans honored the deer or buffalo that were killed to provide meat for the tribe. The spirit of the animal was honored, for without the animal to kill, the tribe could not survive. The spirituality of the connection to the animals was clearly revealed in the shamanic use of animals in healing and wisdom quests. Shamans also shape-shifted to strengthen their abilities to attract food for the tribe. For example, shamans would connect to the minds of the buffalo and direct the herd to an area that was favorable for the hunters. I have used this shape-shifting technique to become a small fish and swim into the channels of the body to find blockages. Our minds hold all these connections; it is visualization that makes use of the knowledge.

I leave you with this thought: Be kind to animals. They may have been your brother, or sister, or mother, or father, in a past life.

Chapter 7

House Clearing

House clearing gets rid of most of the low-level toxic waste that has built up in an enclosed environment. Thoughts, energies, entities, curses, hexes, and more, as listed at the end of this chapter, all leave a residue of disorganized energy that coats anything exposed, just as tar coats the lungs of a smoker. We are just now coming to an understanding of this effect. As an energy worker, I clear houses and buildings of that toxic residue and set the intent that no more residues will clog the environment so cleared. I also give strategies to ensure that potential residue sources are discouraged from re-entering. In addition, I encourage homeowners to protect themselves from negative thoughts that some guest might try to leave behind by brushing the thoughts out the door with the departing guest.

Examples of House Clearings

House clearings have presented some interesting occurrences. A house on Cape Cod contained 93 ghosts, not inside the house itself but on the property on which the house was built. Further information revealed that a tribe of Native Americans had been massacred on the land upon which the house was built. The 93 souls were locked in the trauma of that horror and had been reliving the event over and over for hundreds of years. My guides and angels were able to assist these 93 souls to make the journey to the appropriate dimension.

While on the Cape, I went to a presentation by an author of a book about ghosts of Cape Cod. He speculated that in some locations, it was hard to determine the true identity of the ghost. I told him that such information could be discovered easily enough. Any medium, myself included, could nail down the question with a simple contact.

I made just such a contact in a house in Hyde Park. The clearing I was doing for the owners revealed that ten ghosts were in residence. The owners expressed a desire to work with some of the ghosts. I asked if it was appropriate that some ghosts remain here. I received information that three of the ten would be willing to work with the owners. The other seven were sent on their way to the next dimension. The remaining three I interviewed and introduced to the owners.

Josh was 17 when he drowned in the river behind the house. He loved the stream and the woods around the house. He had been opening and closing doors at random, which was how the owners experienced his presence. He was also very fond of the resident cats and, in addition, would create temperature changes in the rooms. He had a mischievous streak and would move things around. He was very eager to be known.

The next resident soul was a little girl who had been aborted in a small hut on the property. She appeared to be about five years old when I met her. This and similar contacts have changed my understanding of abortion. The soul as energy exists before birth and can become lost at any point. She was very interested in all the goings-on in the house and liked to involve herself in the cooking and tested all the creations of the kitchen.

Emily was 22; she loved the gardens. It was she who had insisted that a mirror be added to the bedroom wall. She had died in childbirth long before the present house had been built. I didn't have much time to spend with her but I will go there again and connect with her.

I don't wish to advocate for keeping ghost souls in their present state. I would be the first to wish them well on their journey. The situation that locked them into their position prevents them from moving on in their soul journey. On the other hand, maybe they are here as observers, gaining understanding that eluded them in life. There are no "accidents," so they must be here for some purpose.

A house I cleared in Burlington was set on the edge of the lake. I found layers and layers of former cultures that had left behind thought forms and curses so intense I was weighed down the moment I entered the house. The present owners had learned to live with the heaviness, and did not associate the house's atmosphere with their own unhappiness. My concern was for the grandchild who was brought to visit. All the malfeasance was a tremendous burden for the baby. When I had performed the clearing and removed all the many layers of thoughts and curses, ghosts and hexes, the difference was immediate. I set pins around the house and found that the electrical entrance was a problem. I noted that the use of magnets would offer some relief, and left it to the owners to follow up on this part.

Electricity and Harmony

The electronic age provides all kinds of electrical frequencies that disrupt our own wiring. Cell phones, computers, electric lights, radios, CD players, television, toasters, and all the electric appliances we have come to depend on, offer a variety of frequencies that bombard our own energy fields. Dimmer switches are a silent menace, for they are designed to be on continuously, emitting a low-level impulse. The same is true of television. When our bodies are constantly exposed to such lower frequencies, our normal currents are disrupted. The effect is exacerbated by constant exposure. Like a rock in a stream that changes the flow of water, so is our body's electrical system flow altered.

Nature is a harmonizing frequency. We know that plants convert carbon dioxide and give off oxygen; they also vibrate at a level that is symbiotic to our bodies. Unlike the rock that disrupts the stream, these harmonic frequencies keep our energy flowing at an optimum level.

The Beneficial Effects of Prayer

Studies have shown that prayer has a positive effect on brain cells. The negative effects of curses and hexes are also definable. I have seen the impact of thoughts on drops of water. A thought such as "I hate you," when projected to a drop of water, will cause the molecules of water to disintegrate and disorganize. By the same token, when the thought "I love you" is projected to the water drop, a beautiful pattern emerges, organized and symmetric. I have observed this phenomenon with my own eyes at a Danville Chapter meeting of ASD. The evidence is also available on the Web. I offer this evidence to emphasize the importance of removing the non-beneficial issues from any environment. Environments in which we spend a lot of time are more harmonious if the residue is removed. Places where we sleep, eat, work, and relax in should refresh our brains and bodies, not bombard them with disorganizing residue.

Who and What are Ghosts?

I would like to offer an explanation of the issue of ghosts or poltergeists who may be impacting a house or building. Most ghosts are disorganized baby souls caught between dimensions by trauma and have not been able to disengage from the particular environment. Sick houses, buildings, and property are coated with toxic residue that disorganizes the electrical flow of all living things. That explains why many people feel a ghost's presence rather than see it. Remember that when I refer to a "baby soul," I'm not referring to a chronological age of this lifetime. I refer to number of lifetimes of the soul entity. The baby soul as limited experience of the disengagement from one life to the next. The vessel (body) has finished its existence; however, its electric soul is disorganized. Like the drop of water, the electric soul, when bombarded with trauma or thoughts, becomes disorganized. The soul is not able to make the transition, so it stays caught in the dimension between here and there. This scenario plays out from the simplest organism to the grandest plan of the Universe.

When I clear ghosts from a house or piece of land, the guides who work through me literally sweep up all the dissimilated bits and pieces of the baby souls and carry them to the recovery level. It sometimes happens that not all the soul parts are recovered completely. (As Grandfather said, "If we were perfect, we would be on the 33rd level"). Such splintered souls may experience many lifetimes before all the parts are reunited. I do soul retrievals to gather up all the fractured parts of a soul and bring them back into a whole being. Shamans of the world have practiced this art of soul retrieval from antiquity.

I am able to connect with ghosts because of my vibration level, just as I can connect to souls that are in Spirit/Faerie or on other levels in mediumship. My guides and angels have trained my brain for this work, just as a body builder trains the body. Light workers and energy workers all over the world are attempting to clear the toxic residue of hate and darkness that is clogging our environment, our planet Mother Earth.

House-Clearing Rituals

I have a formula that I use when doing clearing work. I work very closely with my dowsing tool, a pendulum. My guides help me answer some prepared questions, which include:

Are there non-beneficial energies possessing this house/ building? Yes/No
How many?
How strong?
Can we clear these now?

Are there non-beneficial entities present? Yes/ No
How many?
How strong?
Can we clear them now?

Are there noxious rays present? Yes/No
How many?
How strong?
Can we clear them now?

Are there curses or hexes in effect? Yes/No
How many?

How strong?
Can we clear these now?

Are there low-level beings present? Yes / No
How many?
Can we clear these now?

Are there non-beneficial frequencies present? Yes / No
How many?
How strong?
Can we clear these now?

Are there non-beneficial thought forms in effect? Yes / No
How many?
Can we clear these now?

Are there non-beneficial energies present that are affecting the house/
    building or property? Yes / No
How many?
Can we clear these now?

Are there non-beneficial influences, not within the confines of the house/
building or property? Yes / No
How many?
Can we clear these now?

Are there ghosts or poltergeists affecting the house/building
    or property? Yes / No
How many?
Can we clear these now?

What percentage of available life force is here?
If less than 60 percent, we make an effort to increase the percentage.

What is the percentage of energy level? Yes / No
If less than 60 percent, we make an effort to increase the percentage.
What is the love level percentage?
If less than 60 percent, we make an effort to increase the percentage.

Is underground water an issue here? Yes / No
If Yes, then we may try to divert the water.

Are electric lines an issue here? Yes / No
If Yes, magnets may work to divert the electric issue.

Are lay lines affecting this house/building or property? Yes / No
If Yes, we may divert the lay lines if appropriate.

Vortexes and water domes are also checked.

Some of the houses I have cleared using this format have revealed issues outside this range. One in particular, had been cleared by four different individuals. I said I would try to see what they missed. My guides said I could do it. To my great amazement, I found the problem to be an energy ray that was directed to the ground under the house from another dimension. The house was just in the way. I was directed to put a barrier around the house so the ray was deflected around the house. As with everything, you start with a form; then be willing to think outside that form if it doesn't seem to be working.

Chapter 8

Karma

You have probably heard many things about "karma." It is a term found in Hinduism and Buddhism related to the force generated by a person's actions to perpetuate transmigration. In its ethereal consequences, karma determines the soul's destiny in the next existence. It has to do with vibration levels. In this chapter, I will try to unravel the misunderstandings of karma in the cosmic plan.

Karma is the destiny to which the soul aspires. It is the experience that will raise the vibration and make us one with the Source. Karmic lessons are both dark and light in equal measure so that the soul learns to be objective, not subjective. The soul must learn to experience events without making ego-based judgments, without deeming something "good" or "bad." Once the cord that attaches judgment to a situation is cut, the soul can vibrate in the angel realms. As more and more souls achieve such vibrations, mankind will evolve to the next vibration level.

When working with clients, I use a chart to dowse their karmic progress in this lifetime. Readings change as lessons are learned and goals are reached. Negative karma readings mean the client may have some unpleasant lessons yet to learn in this lifetime. The chart runs from negative 100 to plus 100, and gives a reference point to a soul's place on its life path.

The soul family incarnates to help the soul learn the karmic lessons that were agreed upon before this lifetime was started.

These lessons are found on the scroll lodged in the Hall of Contracts, which is a long, low building located at the -09 level on my map of the upper and lower levels in the back of this book. I have traveled to that level and seen my own contract. The word I found there was "TWIN." At first I didn't understand that this meant that Carter and I are twin flames, though now I have gained insight with much contemplation and revelation.

In a past lifetime, Carter had cut off my fingers. This created karma between us. To balance this karma, I would need to cut off his fingers in this lifetime, which I don't want to do. To circumvent that karmic action, I had to request permission to a change the rule of karma. Karma is a High God Law, and only the Godhead can grant such a request. I asked that this karma between Carter and me be commuted to something positive, and my wish was granted.

I also asked for a change in karma for my children. Again, it meant requesting permission, for it involved a High God Law, and again, my wish was granted. This may sound easy, but it is not. Changing karma has weakened me physically. I once enjoyed good health and now have afflictions that have altered my life. I am learning from this and try to remain an objective observer. I perform daily healing rituals. Let me say that playing with karma isn't cool and it should be done only after great consideration.

Karma for me in this lifetime has meant that I had to endure a 25-year marriage to an alcoholic abuser. During my most recent past life, I was a wine grower in France and had abused my wife. In this lifetime, karmic destiny required that I had to experience the exact opposite situation.

I have heard it said that no new souls would start the journey to the Source. That is likely true. The original count of souls was 80,000, according to antiquity. There are many times that number now coming and going on Earth. We see the havoc this population has wreaked on this planet. The God Plan is to assist the beings on Earth in evolving to their next soul levels. The purpose of karma is to provide the soul with lessons from lightness and darkness equally. The premise is that a being can not fully understand true unconditional love unless that being has experienced the diametrical opposite: true hate and despair. That is why a killer in one lifetime becomes the victim in the next lifetime. Thus, as we move into a position of operating from unconditional love, I have read, the issue of karma may begin to change.

The karma-guided soul will, over the course of one thousand lifetimes more or less, have the opportunity to experience vast amounts of information. All this information has been stored in our brains, a huge database. I have dealt with people who are experiencing the negative effects from things that happened in past lives. A karmic issue may intrude into the present, for if a traumatic event has happened in the past, that information is still stored in our vast brain database. If the person is still traumatized, the issue can cause distress in the present lifetime.

Soul Splintering

One of the effects of such karmic trauma might be "soul splintering," when one or more parts of the soul retreats to a safe place. This happens to ensure that a soul is not totally destroyed. For instance, when a child is physically abused, that child may not have a safe place to go. The physical body must suffer the pain. The soul, however, is a different element and can leave the physical body to ensure its survival. Part of the soul remains to learn the karmic lesson, while another part retreats to a safe place.

Someone once asked me if a soul incarnates "complete," meaning with all its parts together. In some cases, the answer is no. If, for instance, the parts of a soul have not been retrieved in a past life, the soul remains splintered, even through the transmigration referred to as death. The soul might not even be aware that the splintering took place. The pathway to that particular memory file is blocked. This is why victims may be in therapy for years and still not improve. Many energy workers experience the intense emotions of clients who have had such blockages removed. True healing can happen only when the soul has re-established itself in its entirety, and the splinters are united in one unit again.

The Big Picture of Karma

Karma operates on many levels. Even the galaxies operate with karma; the relationships of the galaxies are ruled by karma. Birth, death, the growth of stars, are controlled by the Lords of Karma. You will find their location on my map (List of 33) in the last chapter.

Far in the past, Earth was battered by another planet during a battle of galactic proportion. Evidence of this battle can be seen in the flat bottom of the Pacific Ocean and the asteroid belt that surrounds the Earth. The collision that occurred knocked the bits of the planet into space as asteroids. Because of their connection to this planet, the asteroids revolve around the Earth, serving both as protection and containment. The asteroid belt protects Planet Earth from attack by other space bodies, for the deflection they pose wards off would-be intruders and invaders. The asteroids also prevent the planet from wandering off to do battle elsewhere in the galaxies. While this information might seem strange to you, it expresses the understanding that all things are connected and part of the whole. We humans are not some isolated life form existing in a vacuum. From the ground we walk to the heaven we admire, energy is the binding force.

Just as our bodies are comprised of subatomic particles, so is the infinite vast space of galaxies, which too is made up of subatomic particles. Our bodies are working models, microcosms of the vastness of the galaxy. For instance, our bodies take the base particles and divide those into cells, which in turn become body parts that operate independently of one another, yet form part of one entity. Similarly, the galaxy takes base particles, creates independent yet dependent parts, as one single entity. Quantum physicists, eat your heart out! Who knew?

Karma is the High God Law that governs creation, from the individual soul to vast, unlimited space. However, just as evolution occurs on all levels, karma is destined to evolve and change. I have heard of such changes and experienced change for myself. I will not speculate the outcome of this change here, though lightworkers the world over are making such projections. Simply put, just as man evolves, so will karma.

Chapter 9

Field Notes

This chapter shares some of the work I have done over the years.

Specialized Spirit Guides

I did a program at a local college for the student activity committee last night. To my great surprise, one of the readings I did brought in "Gray Feather" as one of a young man's spirit guides. I asked if he was a writer. He responded that some of his teachers had encouraged him to write. I think he was doing computer game development as a major. The reason I asked about writing is that Gray Feather is a well-known spirit guide for writers whom I had encountered during a reading I did in Glen Falls, New York , where the client was a writer. Also, Rosemary Altea wrote a book called *The Eagle & the Rose;* her spirit guide was Gray Feather. I find it very interesting that spirit guides appear to specialize in different fields like that. Clearly the young college man has a great teacher with him to guide his growth. For me, as a medium, it was like seeing an old friend.

Another of the students was amazed that I could describe his Grandpa Max to him as a rotund man sitting in a chair with a pet in his lap. The pet was a parrot that had lived to be 96 years old. The grandfather was artistic but could only do art as a hobby.

When I then asked the young man if he was working on a painting. The message he got through me was that the focus was not clear in this painting. He then told me that he had an old postcard of the building where his Grandpa Max had worked; one part of the card was damaged and he had not been able to create that part. I told him that if he asked for help from Max, the insight would come.

Harnessing the Power of the Mind

I was visiting one of my daughters; it was the first time I had stayed in her home. The bed was set against the outside wall under the window and the door to the room was about twelve feet from the bed. As I lay there with my eyes open, I suddenly saw waves of air flowing rhythmically toward me from the doorway like some huge bird swimming through the air. I knew immediately that I was seeing Carter's energy coming toward me. The wave continued until it totally enfolded me and I was held in the power of his energy. It was mesmerizing, terrifying, and awe-inspiring all at the same time. The visual confirmation of the intensity of his mind-power is embedded in my consciousness. That visualization proves the power of the mind that all of us have access to if we can learn to control and focus that power.

Soul Retrieval

My soul retrieval work has provided interesting experiences as well. One particular client had two soul parts that we searched for. We found one part on the 30th level with a lovely and graceful star being; that soul part was of Pleiadean ilk. When doing soul retrievals, I use my dowsing tool to determine which soul parts to look for, and then use my map to locate the splintered parts. I then go to retrieve the parts and integrate them with the rest of the soul. The important element is then to ensure that the retrieved parts remain together. I have created, with the help of one of my clients, a ritual listed in the back of the book to encourage the soul parts, once united, to remain intact.

On Adoption

One encounter I had involved a young woman who wished to speak with another woman in the spirit realm. I immediately got the message that that person was not related to the client I was reading for. When I gave this information to the confused client, she told me it was her older sister. Wondering why I would have been given misinformation, I again asked if the spirit was related and again the answer came that they were not. When I then asked if adoption was the issue, I got a clear "yes." It was then a question of whether my client or the "sister" had been adopted.

The story that was revealed was this: my client had been adopted at six months. Her birth parents had been killed in an accident. Friends of her parents were caring for my client when the fatal accident occurred. The friends continued to care for her and eventually adopted her. She never knew that she was not born of her adoptive mother. The reason I was sent to give her this news was that her birth parents wanted to meet her. To do that, she needed to know that they were waiting to meet her on the other side.

I asked Dan Churchill about the whole episode, as it was a first for me as a reader. Dan explained that what had occurred was an agreed meeting set up when the birth parents agreed to experience the accident and loss of their child. I was the messenger who would allow their daughter to know of their existence, so they could then contact her.

Along those same lines, I was once reading for a client and kept seeing a baby about six months old sitting in the grass wearing a lovely lace dress. The client couldn't make any connection to this child, so I moved on to a woman who was expressing great love to my client. I described the woman to my client; the message that came through was "You may not have known that I loved you, but I did what I thought was best for you." Still the client could not make any connection. She seemed unable to understand the spirit that was giving the message or what the message meant. I urged my client to write everything down, as I always do with readings so that the understanding might come at a later time. The reading continued, revealing a house with a dark cloud over it. I turned to the client and tears were streaming down her face. I got up to comfort her and hugged her tight. The message was clear to her now and she sobbed out the story that she had been given up for adoption. That was the baby in the reading and the spirit of the woman I had described to her was the birth mother she had never known. The full import of the message she had been given finally revealed itself. The experience was something she never expected.

Life Paths and Choices

I am often asked to give readings of the future. I'm not a fortune-teller. This is a "free will zone" and each soul has a destiny. Our destinies can change, for each choice we make today determines tomorrow's outcome. You have a life path but you can choose not to follow that path. That is free will at work. When doing readings, I can give you possible outcomes but it is up to you to make that outcome happen. For instance, I can talk to Granddad on the other side and he may tell you that the guy you're with is not good for you. In fact Granddad might even say "That guy is no damn good for you." (Granddad's words, not mine). If you don't listen to Granddad and dump the guy, then you have made a conscious choice. That choice will affect the outcomes.

The same is true of many life choices: a business venture, an operation, a relationship. I can get information to help you make informed choices, but if you choose not to heed spiritual guidance, you are putting your free will to work.

Connecting to Souls

I connect to the vibration of souls that are in a different dimension. These souls see the big picture and can offer an objective point of view. They want to help, they are willing to help, but they can only help if you are willing to let them.

The souls I connect with in other dimensions are not ghosts, they are at a time of rest between lifetimes. Ghosts are souls that are caught between dimensions; they should have moved on to the next plane but, for some reason, could not make the transition. In some cases, it is trauma that holds them. Others have unfinished business. Still others are just plain lost. Sometimes, family bonds are so strong that the soul cannot move on.

"Resting between lifetimes" does not mean they are not learning lessons to raise their awareness. It means that they are evaluating the level they are at and making choices for the next time around in an atmosphere of oneness and total love. These souls still maintain a connection to the soul family they spent the last past life with. I connect to their vibrations. In the readings that I do, I usually ask the name of the person the client wishes to speak to so that we can best utilize the time available. If the client doesn't know any one in particular who has crossed over, then I can "cruise" to see which soul or souls have a message for the client. I usually go to "Spirit /Faerie" (level 05). If the soul I seek is not there, I will use my map to dowse where they might be found. Occasionally the person/soul I seek is not available.

I once did a reading and connected a client with her uncle, who gave her a message. The next day we tried to again make the connection with the uncle and he was unavailable. He was in seclusion reviewing with his guides what he would work on in his next life cycle. It usually happens that a recently crossed over soul is in recovery for a certain period of time. The amount of time a soul is in recovery varies with the trauma surrounding the crossover. Such trauma could be mild or horrendous, depending on the circumstances. It is usually a good idea to wait, at least six to eight weeks before attempting to connect with a soul who has crossed over.

At a Mind and Body Expo in Hyannis, on Cape Cod, Massachusetts, an older woman sat down with me. She assured me that she didn't believe in any of this, but her daughters had insisted that she get a reading. I asked whom she wish to contact on the other side. Her son, she replied. I said he liked to collect antique cars. She looked incredulous. I told her that he was sending her a flower, a calla lily. Then she told me a story: She had painted a picture of her son after he passed over and had gone all over town to find a calla lily to put into the picture with her son. "I didn't think he ever knew," she said. "He knew," I said, and the woman went away a believer.

Where Does Life Begin?

There are times that I connect to young children on the other side. Sometimes they are souls who were aborted in this lifetime, who then connect to the mother and offer forgiveness and love. These incidences have changed my feelings as to when life really starts. I now understand that the choice to live is made long before the birth event. It may be that karma makes the choice on both sides. Mother and child are just vessels. As an aside, I believe the advocates of "pro-choice" or "pro-life" are just whistling in the wind. What goes down is out of their hands. They are operating from ego-based, judgments. Unconditional love is expressed when no judgment is made and the event is experienced as an event without blame.

Maintaining Connections

There is a lady in New York state who comes to see me to connect with her young daughter who passed over. Heather, the daughter, always sends rainbows and stars to her mother. These moments are precious to both. The child can reassure her mother that she is happy, busy, and that her love is strong. The mother can maintain a connection to ease the pain of separation until she is ready to let go. I am honored to be the medium who can maintain this tenuous connection for them.

Our Physical Bodies

I come from a shaman venue, meaning that I believe in the body's ability to heal itself. The body was not created in perfection just to have it break down .The breakdown that occurs is self-inflicted. When I read clients' auras in my energy work, I feel these physical issues as hot spots on the body. I also get messages intuitively if I am working long distance.

A simple example: Johnny has a test at school that he really doesn't want to take. The thought of taking the test makes him "uneasy." (He is in a state of dis-ease). He tells his mom he has a stomach ache. This is a created physical issue to avoid the test. It works! Mom says he doesn't have to go to school. The pattern is set: stomach ache, no school. Dis-ease now becomes an avoidance mechanism. Once this thought pattern takes form, it can have a destructive impact on the physical body.

The above is a simple example of how breakdown can occur on the physical level. A mantra: *Thought precedes action.* The thought of breakdown always precedes the physical result. For instance, women who believe they will get cancer draw that dis-ease to them. The physical result starts as a thought: "I will get cancer." That thought organizes in the brain until just the word creates a response of fear in the physical body, which then releases chemicals to corroborate that end result. Cancer in and of itself didn't become an epidemic. The "fear of cancer" is the epidemic. Fear is an ego-based, self-realizing prophecy. Once we give thought to a fear, it has the power to manifest in our physical lives simply because we created it. The same is true about fear of any kind.

Healing Thoughts

I have experienced the power of healing. I once had a severe pain in my left side. I was doubled over with it. I finally said to the universal power: "Enough! This pain is unacceptable. I want it gone NOW!" To my utter amazement, I felt a bubble the size of a grapefruit at the site of the pain. As I continued to refuse the pain, the bubble exited my body through my back and took with it the severe pain. It worked! I will add that I was lying on an air mattress when the bubble left my back; following this event, the mattress lost all its air as a physical sign of the power of the bubble I exorcized from my body.

If you believe you must live in pain because you feel you deserve it, that is ego-based thinking. Our brains are so powerful they will create what we want. If, as a child, you were bombarded with negative thoughts about your worth, such thoughts manifest in action once your brain has accepted these valuations.

Religion through the ages has told us we are born in sin. WHAT AN ABSOLUTE LIE! We are BORN IN ABSOLUTE PERFECTION! The "God's image" part is correct: we can create or destroy, for we have free will. The choice of creation or destruction is a judgment call; judgment is an ego-based view, just like fear.

You may be thinking: what about people who are born with issues of disability? Disabilities may be karmic issues. Souls who lived in a perfect body in one lifetime may choose to experience a less-perfect vessel in a subsequent lifetime to experience both sides of the issue for their soul growth. Remember, "disability" is a judgment and, as such, is ego-based. What you may perceive as a disability may in fact give a different perspective for the soul inhabiting that body.

Speaking of health, I think this is the time to mention heart issues. Heart disease is one of the major health issues in this country. This situation has come about as a result of putting too much stress on the heart as the loving emotion center of the body. We refer to such conditions as "heartache," "broken-hearted," "heartsick," "wearing one's heart on one's sleeve," and "heart attack," to name but a few. All these non-beneficial expressions put tremendous strain on the poor heart muscle. The heart is a pump; it is not the emotional center we confuse it with.

Let me tell you about the chakras, for they too are important to understanding health. The seven major chakras line up on the frontal mid-line of the body. These are the root chakra, the sacral chakra, the solar plexus chakra, the heart chakra (located at a mid-line point over the thymus gland, which was indeed designed to be the emotional "heart center" of the body), the throat chakra, the third-eye chakra over the pineal gland, and the crown chakra. Each of these major power centers of the body connects to a specific gland. These glands all have the strength to handle chemical responses unleashed by highly charged emotions.

I'm sure you have heard of people, who at times of trauma, have performed feats of unbelievable proportion. This is the work of the adrenal glands, which can suffuse the body with amazing strength by pumping out adrenalin. This same adrenalin over time can wear away the lining of the intestines, as seen in the effect of prolonged exposure to physical and emotional abuse.

Our glands can handle very strong currents, for that is their purpose. If we are going to move to a place of unconditional love, we must place the work of the heart center where it belongs: in a gland that was designed to handle the intensity of electrical and chemical responses that center commands, namely the thymus. Leave the poor pump to its job of maintaining circulation. Once we have made this shift in perception, the number of broken hearts, heartaches, and feelings of heartsickness will go down dramatically.

We all have the power to shift the heart center of the body to the thymus gland. We can do it several different ways, as shown on the following page:

A. Cleanse the individual chakras:
   - Find a calm place
   - Take three deep cleansing breaths
   - Relax, visualizing the crown chakra as a pail of liquid on your head
   - Tip your head forward and empty everything out of that pail, asking Mother Earth to transmute all that liquid in love. Once the pail is empty, close the crown chakra and seal it with a rose or a cross.

B. Now visualize the third-eye chakra. Open it, again as a pail full of a liquid. Bend forward and empty everything out of the pail, asking Mother Earth to transmute all the liquid in love. Once the pail is empty, close the chakra with a cross or a rose.

C. The throat chakra can be cleaned in the same way. Be sure to close up the chakra after cleaning.

D. Then we come to the thymus (heart center). Proceed with the cleaning as before to the point of closing. Here you can place intent on the thymus as the emotional heart center by saying: "I ask to shift my physical heart center to the thymus heart chakra." Continue to close the heart chakra. Then complete the rest of the cleaning of the last three chakras.

E. It would be well to continue this shifting of intent periodically until you feel a change in the point at which you feel your loving emotion at the thymus rather than in the heart pump. If you are a dowser, you can ask if the shift has been completed. You may wish to try palpating the thymus and putting intent that your heart center reside there. The information I get is that cleaning out the chakras first is the most effective way to accomplish the desired shift.

Let me share an event related to the heart. Once, I started to experience an attack of the heart. My chest began to constrict and I became short of breath. I knew my blood pressure was rising. I called to my medical guides/angels and headed straight to my bed, where I turned on a relaxation tape and began to slow my breathing down. I called on Archangel Michael to help me. I could feel the warm vibration of love from my guides/angels. I closed my eyes and willed myself to absorb that vibration, and to let go and rely entirely on their help to bring me through this event. Archangel Michael had told me I would go through the "valley of the shadow" and I did.

I mention this event to express the idea that once we eliminate ego-based fear and accept an experience as just that—"an experience"—without judgment as to good or bad, we are more likely to come through the "valley" safely. Even if you put your life in the hands of a doctor, when you can come from a place without fear, you will be much more likely to have a successful outcome. Fear generates chemical action in the brain, which in turn releases a chemical reaction in the body. That fear suffuses the total body complex with non-beneficial energy. The situation created makes it much harder for the body to heal or to even survive. The body is working in a very unfavorable environment.

Prayer has now been studied; the brain waves generated during prayer have been recorded. The calming effects of prayer result from the brain chemicals that are created and suffuse the body with beneficial energy. This effect allows the body to heal within a beneficial environment, instead of fighting against ego-based fear. During prayer, the body is enveloped in unconditional love. The warm vibration stimulates the body's ability to heal itself.

Just as fear can cause and exacerbate epidemics, unconditional love can quell them. When we accept that, we have the power to use this understanding and take responsibility for our own healing. That is the wisdom of the shaman. It is native wisdom. The shaman made ceremonies that included the whole tribe in the healing work, for such participation invoked the power of love from all the tribe directed to healing the illness. Drums, rattles, and chants all create vibration. The person needing healing was enveloped in the positive energy of unconditional love expressing itself in warm vibrations.

Healing occurred when the body responded with waves of healing energy washing away the non-beneficial energy.

Such healing has been known to us from antiquity. However, just as we have given all our responsibility away, we have given our health away to the doctors, our God away to the priests, our self-determination away to the government, and our knowledge away to the schools. Reasserting our individual power and creativity is a dynamic life change. Once we have eliminated all the scapegoats from our mindset, then we stand alone before the universe and truly become the creators we were meant to be.

That is the God image for which we were created. Loving masters of all we survey, we are creators in unconditional love. We are all one with the "Source." Within each of us is the creator, the power, the healer, the "gnowing." The evolutionary plan is upon us. We are to move to the fourth dimension, from which we will operate from this unconditional love. The curtain will be raised and we will see that we are creators, each of us. The power within is the power without. We are one with the Source, God's image.

This is very important for you to understand. It is the information that light workers, crystal balancers, vibrational tuners, and shamans the world over are tapping into to invoke the positive results they achieve. The problem we encounter in this work is that clients go back to the same environment that generated the dis-ease in the first place; the positive program is bombarded with non-beneficial energies again.

The "Gestalt" theory applies here. To truly experience the beneficial effects of energy work, the environment, as well as the body, respond to the positive flow of energy. Clients can enhance the positive effects of the energy work by using ongoing affirmations and inviting a protective energy to insulate against the environment of non-beneficial energy. House clearing and office clearing can empower positive healing as well.

Water

The water we get from the faucet, if from a communal system, is poisoned with chlorine, fluoride, and all the other additives the general public is convinced are good for us. A healthy body can usually offset the poisons in the "civilized" environment we have created. However, for persons who are emotionally and physically stressed, this environmental hazard can affect the body's ability to heal. The "Gestalt" theory encompasses the whole body and its functioning environment. For what is the body, if not a star within a sphere? Any healing must take into consideration all that "Gestalt" envisions. Even the Western medical community has grasped that concept. For instance, if you caution a smoker about the risk of smoking and operate on the damaged areas of the person's lungs, it will not change the outcome unless the smoker is willing to change the smoking habit that precipitated the issue. This same scenario is true of most healing venues.

Meditation in Healing

One of the first steps to healing is meditation. Even if you don't have much time, the effect can be maximized. Find a quiet place and just take a few deep breaths. Close your eyes and invite your place of authority to manifest. The resulting oxidation of the body will give a feeling of well-being that enhances the healing process in all the seven layers of consciousness. Outer and inner stressors will be handled from your place of authority. You will begin to act, instead of react, to your inner and outer environment. Once you have dedicated a meditative time/space, the beneficial effect you will experience carries over into to all aspects of your life. Our body is our vessel that we ask to operate continually with minimal care. The meditative time/space is for our body to regroup, to reorient, to re-center, to reestablish the chemical balance. When we meditate, we can step back into the life race from a place of authority. We are then able to act in life issues rather than react.

The wonderful aspects of meditation are that there is no expense, no intricate moves, no secret knowledge to which only initiates are privy. Nor do we have to buy special diets. Meditation is a gift that everyone can receive equally. Time and space are the only requirements.

Close your eyes and take a deep breath, and repeat until you have experienced the shift of perception to your heart center (the thymus). You will re-enter the chaos of life from a place of balance and peace. Your center of authority reasserts itself.

I work through my third eye (the pineal gland) when I do readings that connect me to the spiritual realms. It is this gland that responds to the different vibrational amplitudes of other dimensions. I usually "see" the forms of other vibrational dimensions in black and white, because often the sender (spirit) is unable to vibrate in color. Only rarely do I see colors, though on occasion I have. Most of my readings have a time limitation, which may be part of the issue; a longer connection time might allow the spirit sender to rev up to a color mode. The energy expended even for the five or ten minutes of connection is very intense. That is why most encounters involve a message from the spirit to assure the client that in fact the client is known to the spirit and that the spirit is able to help with a problem the client is facing or will face. I can carry out these readings in great halls with mass distractions or in small rooms with minimal noise; the same concentration is required either way. I am often asked if I need a quiet place to do my readings, and the answer is no! I connect to the vibrations of the spirit like plugging in a cord to an electrical outlet. Once the connection is made, the energy flows, regardless of the activity in the area.

Chakra Connections

There is a beautiful connection that can be achieved through the chakra centers of the body. I would suggest it be done with a person who is very close to you. It is so powerful a connection that it should not be enacted lightly. The opening of the chakra centers of the body and mingling them with a partner's energy centers can surround the bodies with a vibration of exquisite dimension that is powerful enough, when combined with un-conditional love, to elevate the participants to a different reality.

I will explain the elements of the exercise: Start by sending unconditional love to your partner. When you come into close proximity to each other, ceremoniously begin opening the en-ergy centers of your body, starting at the root chakra. Visualize an orange fountain of light emanating from each of you at the same time. This fountain of orange color mingles and surrounds you both.

Then open the sacral chakra. This light will be red. Allow the orange and red to join in a splash of vibrant color all around your bodies. The yellow of the solar plexus then springs forth and you will start to really feel the pull of the energy that is re-leased at that moment. Your bodies then become one with the vortex of energy that is generated by the chakras; red, or-ange ,and yellow bands of color hold you fast.

Then the heart chakra of green is opened. The crescendo of energy and the color of that energy form a bond of uncondi-tional love that can literally carry you to another dimension. Then the blue of the throat chakra is opened and the indigo of the third eye (pineal gland) is added. Open now the white gold of the crown chakra. A rainbow of color and energy sweeps and spins in and out and around your bodies. This convergence of two energy bodies could become so intense that you are transported into a parallel universe.

After you have experienced this union, your physical bodies will be tired and you will want to keep hydrated. Be sure to go back and close each chakra center and seal with a symbol of your choosing (cross, rose, reiki sign, or infinity), whatever feels right for you. The importance of closing the chakras is to prevent energy from leaking out. Once you have experienced this exercise, you may well grasp the infinite power of creation first hand. I'm very sure you will never have felt so close to another person. The intimate nature of this energy work compels caution as to your partner of choice.

Affirmations

Energy work is very powerful. I have stated that "thought precedes action." Spoken words are the next most powerful tool. Affirmations are the spoken expression of thought and, as such, they can manifest change. Almost any motivational speaker will encourage you to make daily affirmations. Set your goal and speak your goal every day, and the universe will respond. That is part of your creator power. I told you earlier cancer could manifest if you voice the thought that you will get it. Similarly, your creative power can manifest when you speak the affirmation of your personal goals. Don't get bogged down in how the goal will come about; just accept that it will. You have asked, and the universe will answer.

The complexity of our lives may overshadow the answer we receive and we may not even realize that we have been given a response until we pause to contemplate the path our life has taken. We may go through a traumatic upheaval and put a negative light on it only to find, on later scrutiny, that what at the time seemed a breakdown, was ultimately an awakening to a new and wonderful adventure. Out of chaos comes order. Just as birth can be a trauma, the ensuing life is a marvel. The truly amazing information here is that this "chaos to order" part of the creative puzzle operates on all levels—from the vastness of the Universe to the minutest single-celled protozoan, and even to the sub-atomic particles of quantum physics. Energy workers the world over use the powerful energies of thought and word to bring about change on a client level and on a planetary level.

I will inject a milder form of enlightenment here. I have been privileged to work with Archangel Metatron on different occasions. He gave a very interesting and timely message during a channeling session in which I participated. We were seated in a circle and Archangel Metatron was speaking: "Those of you on my right see me from the right side, those of you on my left see a slightly differ-ent view of my left side, and those in the front see a still different view. Yet I am the same on all sides: right, left, front, or back. So it is with many things in life: the focus is the same, only the view or perspective is different." That message was very profound. It ex-pressed the situation of the wars being waged in other parts of the world. The protagonists and antagonists are neither right nor wrong; they simply view things from a different perspective. We see this on a personal level in many aspects of human interaction.

I have invited Archangel Metatron to help us in a table-tipping game. He graciously attended our party of four at the ASD conven-tion at Lyndon State College during a table-tipping workshop. It is a fun exercise where groups of people sit around small tables with their hands flat and resting lightly on top of the table. The angels, guides, and ascended masters were invited to participate in the fun. When my table group was assembled, I asked for Metatron to join us; the table then tipped once for yes, twice for no. We used the letters of the alphabet to ascertain who our guest was. I had asked for Archangel Metatron, so as soon as we presented the letter M and got a yes, I was sure it was he/she. I then asked to confirm if it was he and got another "Yes." The Archangel wanted to give us a message but the time of the workshop ran out before we could get the message. In a similar fashion, I called on Archangel Metatron at a small private party, and was grateful that once again, he put in an appearance. This dedication to each soul that asks is very reassuring even in a rather frivolous setting.

Connecting with Star Beings

In another chapter, I mentioned that I had given some names to the Counsel on the 30th level of people who wanted to make contact with star beings. When I heard back from "Peace2U," she described her encounter just so: "The men in black," as they called themselves, worked to teach her to astral travel. They patiently coached her as she attempted to take flight. They would get her into the air , but then, being her own worst enemy, she would look down and immediately crash back to ground. She said they gently helped her become airborne again and again. They finally said they would be back and assured her she had done well for her first time.

Banu from Turkey also experienced an encounter. She had had some experience with astral travel so they took her on a journey to a distant star. They also showed her how to use the silver cord to change places in a parallel dimension.

There were others on the list who had had some contact, but fear prevented them from exploring the possibilities. I have said before that ego-based fear is the single most prevalent issue that hampers interaction with the inhabitants of the Universe.

I have worked with people who have had contact. One man, from childhood on, had seen a black-robed figure at his bedside. His unfounded fear prevented him from experiencing the teachings this gentle being was prepared to impart to him. The man instead manifested a debilitating pain in his hip that was a holdover from a past-life karma. The black-robed figure would have been prepared to work through this karma issue and relieve the pain had he been allowed to. The fear that prevented the healing was finally resolved in later life with the help of a couple of psychics, myself included.

On Religion

Why is fear so destructive? Death is just a transformation to another dimension. We are all angels at the soul level, born in absolute perfection. So why has ego-based fear so permeated our existence?

Religion generates fear to prostrate the population and maintain control. One example of such control is the changing of the musical scale in the early church. The original chants were so powerful and healing that the entire scale was modified to dissipate that power. The Christians changed the words of the holy trinity from "The Father, the Mother, and the Son" to "the Father, Son, and Holy Ghost," virtually eliminating women from the concept all together.

Pagan religions were matriarchal in nature, for they honored the mother above all as the producer of progeny. The family was the base unit and fertility was to be honored. It was fear of the power of the mother that led religious factions to suppress women in religious roles. Only men could be priests, elders and the like.

It seems a bit ridiculous, seeing that each soul experiences both male and female lives in alternating sequence. If you're a man in this life, you were a woman the last time around. Suppression of either sex is self-defeating. Whatever dictates you enact in one lifetime, you will have to live with next time around. That is part of the karmic lessons.

On Government

Governments maintain a fear-based control of the world by following the philosophy of "My gun's bigger than yours." In fact, fear is the reason government exists at all. One person feels he cannot stand against another, so he gets all his friends together and forms a government to protect the individuals from whatever might generate a threat. The difficulty results when the government starts running the individual, instead of the other way round. The government, of course, uses fear of reprisal to maintain control. This only adds to the ego-based fear that permeates our existence.

On Racism

Think for a moment about how much of life is fear-based. We dress a certain way so that others will like us, even respect us. A person of a different culture that dresses in his or her own way is feared, or at least held out of the inner circle. A teen may be feared if he has a colorful lock of hair on his otherwise shaved head. Perhaps he is a Rhodes scholar or honor-roll student, but he looks different and is therefore feared. The same is true of race; the color of skin evokes a certain mindset that must be overcome to overcome the fear. I repeat here: Fear is a self-fulfilling prophecy. The fear that we project to the races is mirrored back to us; because we created it, we made it happen. We wanted it, so it is manifested by us just as we wished it.

Now let's create the reverse. We are all born in absolute perfection. We have all lived lives as different races: black, brown, yellow, red, and white, even as extra-planetary beings. You got that. We have all, at the soul level, lived lives in other cultures, countries, and universes. This information has been disconnected from our memories, but it is still seated deep in the warrens of the brain. This information is the reason that, at this point in evolution, we have the capability to embrace the fourth and fifth dimensions. Once the veil of ego-based fear is lifted from our minds, and we accept that we are all born in absolute perfection, we can step into the enlightened state that awaits us—that of "Unconditional Love."

Unconditional Love / Old Souls

First, we must think: "Unconditional Love." Thought precedes action. The action will become our reality. We are all creators "in God's image." We are one with the Source. Many of the souls on Earth at this time are old souls, meaning that they have had a thousand or more lifetimes on earth and other planets. Old souls have experienced ego-based fear in all its forms over countless lives and they are aware that there is a better way. It is now time for the evolutionary shift to "Unconditional Love."

Soul Cycles

To understand the experience of a soul, think of a drop of water that falls as rain from the cloud in the sky. That raindrop soaks into the ground. A plant growing nearby sucks that drop of water up into its roots, to the stem and the leaves. During the process, the water interacts with the plant to provide life. The plant can reproduce and more life is created. The drop of water is vaporized by the leaf into a mist that evaporates and becomes part of a new cloud, and the process is repeated all over again, all over the world. The soul experiences similar cycles in an energetic form.

There are numerous examples of the cycles of life all around us. The death of plants at the end of a growing season provides fertile ground from which to sprout new life again in spring. Doesn't it just make sense that our own lives follow this pattern life, death and rebirth? We know now that even the vast cosmos operates with this cycle: stars are born and stars die. Order becomes chaos, and chaos becomes order. Those are the dictates of the universe. We are the souls of the Universe.

The many souls on earth at this convergence now have the multiple experiences needed to seek unconditional love on earth as it is in angel realms. These souls know that such an existence is possible. Each time a soul leaves the earth vessel and returns to the angel realms, that soul is reunited with the Source. Once in the angel realms, the most recent, as well as all past lifetimes, are reviewed. The dark side of the soul knowledge has spent itself; there is no future in it the darkest deeds have not brought the sought-after results.

Power has been amassed; conspirators have foisted their control over the unsuspecting masses. To what purpose? One soul seeking control over the world? To amass a huge sum of money? To control the cosmos? To master the game? To become God? This can't happen because we are all God. We are all part of the Source. Each and every soul is a part of the Source. We are already "there." The legendary 300 who seek world dominance are whistling in the wind, playing out games of "chutes and ladders" on a global scale. They may as well bang their heads against the wall or rock back and forth like savants. When they have done their worst—implemented the "protocols" for world dominance—what then? Each member of the SOSM or any other conspiratorial society, the 300, whatever they choose to call themselves, are no different from any other soul experiencing a lifetime on this earth planet. They may experience a "God complex," they may feel they can do a much better job of running things than the present system. Yet each of these individual souls, no matter what group they espouse, has only this lifetime: one birth, one death, in each lifetime, just like every other soul on earth. When their reign of terror on earth ends and they rejoin the Source, what then? It's all so plain and simple. The Illuminati, the 300, and the other secret societies believe that only they can create an acceptable world. They choose to do it by controlling the population and forcing their doctoring on humanity. That is the worldview from the dark side. The dark side doesn't work. It has no future. The ultimate end is total destruction. Then what? What good are fortunes if there is nothing to buy? What good is power if there is no one and nothing to control?

Heaven on Earth

We are in the "garden." Every soul incarnated at this moment is from the Source, created in God's image. We are all creators, from the poorest to the richest. We can create darkness or we can create light. The darkness is chaos, the light is order. We have explored the darkness. What of the light? Where does that lead?

The question then becomes: can we create a heaven on Earth? Yes, we can! Once the light illuminates the dark places, there is nowhere to hide. Darkness is exposed for what it is: just an experience of possible outcomes that must be endured in order to understand the light. The light offers limitless possibilities, for it brings unconditional love, order, and harmony with the cosmos. We can travel beyond the boundaries of space because there is no fear, nothing to box us in and control thought or deed. The tree that we can see from the ground up is mirrored in the tree that lies below our vision. So it is with the universe. What we perceive is expanded exponentially.

Once we accept that we are creators, "in God's image," one with the Source, the "garden" is open to us all. Everyone can see the angels once the veil is lifted. The worldview from the light side asks that all humanity accept its creativity status as "Godlike" and operate from a place of unconditional love. The heaven we all seek is right here in this "garden." We are one with all things. New science is finally revealing the universal truth that was told in the earliest texts and corrupted by special interest groups to enslave the population.

Understand that there is no sin. That is a judgment. What have judgment or punishment really gotten us? They have created a sub-culture of misfits. Crime, destruction, and torture are all dark forces that seek to create a one-world order borne on the backs of human slaves. The criminal elite are holding court. By this I don't mean only the obvious, like the Mafia and organized crime known to operate with immunity all over the world. I am talking about the more stealthy elite that run governments, the secret societies of the medical-military complex, the cancer research centers that mask biological weapons of genocide. These truly represent the dark side.

How can we bring the light into this dark and dangerous situation? The angels know what we are up against. They (we) have agreed to incarnate on the earth at this time to cause a change in the balance of power. Remember, we have all had lessons from the dark side. Our souls have been the Rosecrucians, the Templars, the Freemasons, the 300, the Nazis, and all the other societies that espouse world domination by the elite. We have asserted our godlike natures on the dark side, along with everyone else.

We have learned the lessons that the dark side teaches: there is a better way. The dark side is a self-destructive box that ultimately feeds upon itself and is destroyed. The way of light is outside the box and open to all possibilities when we operate from unconditional love. The vibrations of that thought form travel out like ripples on a pond, from this planet to the entire galaxy and to infinity. No more box, no more self-destruction. We can then become one with the Source. The goal of heaven on earth can be achieved.

You're probably thinking: "OK, that all sounds good. Now how are we going to effect this change?" Note that God is on our side. That may sound idealistic. After all, most wars, including the present ones, are based on that premise. Remember, too, that our soul growth in each subsequent lifetime has been designed (planned) to allow the experience of dark and light on all levels. The present souls in residence have been operating on the dark side for thousands of years. They are no closer to their goals now than before. Open up to the thought of unconditional love. What can it hurt? Let us say you are persecuted for your beliefs; that's not new. So they put you to death; so what, we all die. Death is just a change in form.

You'll be back and still you will reach for the light. The dark side has done its best to create "godship," but it just hasn't worked. The time is upon us to create "godship" from the light side. We are now operating from a higher vibration, the vibration of love and light. We are at a point in evolution that can support that lighter vibration of unconditional love. The dark side has reigned for decades and still cannot reach its goal. The reason is clear: power corrupts and ultimate power corrupts ultimately. There is no peace when the goals are attempted with subterfuge. How can anyone hold power when that position of power has been gained falsely? All the people who helped become potential enemies. There is no place to hide. No "garden" and no peace, even if every soul on earth is in chains. That is the lesson of the dark side.

Many of the souls incarnate on earth today have learned the lessons of the dark side and are now seeking enlightenment. The revelations long predicted are upon us. Unconditional love will win the day and the future will be a new beginning. Not only will we create "heaven" on earth; the cosmic universe will welcome us in the next millennium. The darkness shall pass away and the dawn of the age of light will prevail.

You may ask how I know these things or what authority gives me this knowledge. I am an Angel. That doesn't make me different. You are an Angel too. I repeat we are all souls (spirits, angels) all in God's image, creators. The spark that is our soul is God within.

Hecate once told me that Carter was very spiritual. I wondered what that meant. The dictionary gives a meaning that relates to a deep religious attachment. That ability to communicate with the spirits of the dead. I do that. I am referred to as a medium. On my first quest outlined in the early chapters of the book, I told of my meeting with Jesus, the Christ of Earth. I also described my experience of the World Trade Center, coming face to face with the Godhead and accepting a contract Carter and I. I wrote of the experience of such deep and unconditional love that Carter and I floated up heavenward to be zapped by a bolt of lightning by the male Godhead. Then asking the angels to help us to vibrate higher and higher until we were wrapped in the Oneness of the female Godhead. These were certainly experiences of ecstasy. They proved the power of unconditional love. I, the insignificant soul that I am, have had the power of Godship. The power that all the dark side seeks.

This is the authority that I invoke when I state that every soul is a God within. That there is no sin for that is judgment. We are born in ABSOLUTE PERFECTION. Once we work from a place of unconditional love, the "Creator" within will manifest "Heaven," right here where we are. The reign of darkness has failed to create Godship. The power of light will and is making Godship, now, here. Death, where is thy sting? Those who would threaten death to punish for failure to kneel to a greater power. Hey! That's been done; you have to come up with something better. Let's do it! Let's try UNCONDITIONAL LOVE, the new drug for the next evolution. How do they say: it's "the new designer drug," as if that gives some class to addiction? I am a soldier in the search for truth. I give you my experience of that truth—it is up to you to choose your path. Come from your place of authority and follow the path to Godship, the path of light and love.

> *I call down the white-gold light of Unconditional Love.*
> *I call it into my head and into my heart and surround my body.*
> *I send that white-gold light of Unconditional Love*
>   *to all Mankind.*
> *Let all feel the warm vibration of Unconditional Love in*
> *their hearts, their hearts, their bodies.*
> *I am Love, the Perfect Love, the Unconditional Love.*

Chapter 10

The Shaman

THE HISTORY OF MEDICINE

2000 B.C. "Here, eat this root."
1000 A.D. "That root is heathen. Here, say this prayer."
1850 A.D. "That prayer is superstition. Here, drink this potion."
1940 A.D. "That potion is snake oil. Here, swallow this pill."
1985 A.D. "That pill is ineffective. Here, take this antibiotic."
2000 A.D. "That antibiotic doesn't work anymore. Here, eat this root."
2010 A.D. "That root is contaminated. Here, practice energy medicine."
— Adapted from Qigong Newsletter

I have mentioned my connection with shaman work at several junctures of this book, for I have done journeywork and energy work related to that shamanic venue. The cover picture is my first experience of a quest in a shamanic journey that introduced me to my teacher and guide. I have joined in journeys led by John Kelly, a local shaman, and others. Shamanic work is a form of guided visualization that offers a way to connect to higher energy and enlightenment. Power animals may appear and give a message or insight regarding a particular problem for which the journeyer is seeking an answer.

Such a journey may be to remind us that all the creatures of the creation have a vital role in the cosmic plan. We can learn from all beings. Animal power can often bring amazing understanding to a problem. Insects have survived from the very earliest of times, long before humans appeared on this planet. What is it that allows them to exist through the ages, through freezing temperatures, extreme heat, and in moderate climates? The wolf is a family creature with great cunning. The bear has great strength and is also able to hibernate his great bulk in winter, assuming a state of suspended animation. That same state of suspended animation has saved drowning victims in cold lakes and rivers. The bear is able to do it every winter, while we are much more limited in our ability. Maybe if we could learn the way of the bear, we might acquire that ability.

Native Americans are tuned into the animal kingdom far more deeply than most others living on this continent. They have continued to rely on shamanic journeywork to advance their connection to Mother Earth and Father Universe. They have ascribed traits to many of the animals and honor these in totem carvings and sacred objects that are worn to transmute the strengths of the animal to the wearer. Animals are also studied to instill balance in the person seeking to identify with a particular attribute of his or her power animal. The sought-after result might be that a very shy person would seek to understand a powerful bear to balance that shy part of the human's personality. He or she, when faced with a challenging situation, such as a meeting with a superior, could call upon the bear to provide great power or presence.

If a very delicate hand is needed for a negotiation situation, the wily fox could be consulted to offer a trail that might lead, in a circuitous manner, to the desired end without giving away the objective. Everyone might think that the intended objective was reached, without being aware of how it exactly happened.

One of the reasons I wanted to address shaman work is that some enlightened souls have disparaged it as inappropriate in the present age. I have asked my angels and guides to clarify this issue, and share that information as I was given. I consulted my angel sister on the 26th level. When I made contact with her there, a table appeared to the left. Five other beings were at the table, each with sheaves of papers before them on the table. I addressed them and asked for information about the shamanic issue. I was told that the shaman way is appropriate for connecting to the animal past that all of us have experienced in other lifetimes as part of our soul growth. The enlightened beings that criticize shaman work feel that we have evolved past that connection and therefore deem it without benefit.

The shaman can offer comfort to the soul even in the modern world. The enlightened souls that refute such a concept feel that we have evolved beyond our past and that self-healing is the only way to enlightenment. The soul experience included and still includes animal experience for a reason: to banish that part of soul evolution is to undermine the basic lessons the soul has learned. Skipping a grade in school may advance the soul but it presents the problem of not experiencing all levels from all angles. There is a downside. The soul evolves through experience; skipping the experience undermines the evolution process. The vibration of that experience is absent from the levels of consciousness.

Just as the Universe passes from chaos to order and back to chaos again, the experience of our animal past is vital to the present evolution. The Shaman maintains a close connection to earth and sky, to the cohesive bond of creation. The opening words of this chapter sum it up very well. We have wandered from the path many times over the centuries, yet the path remains. Through reincarnation, the soul experiences life from many vessels (bodies). The slave has been the master, the killer has been the victim, the object has been the subject. We may glorify some potion, some pill, or some new juju, but the path is there throughout all the ages. The ability to tap into the sacred knowledge of the Universe is available to the shaman and the people who seek the truth from all cultures.

The shaman was the first psychotherapist. He or she could connect to an ego-based fear and find the path that would allow healing to take place. Dis-ease starts as a thought; that thought becomes a worry and the worry escalates to manifestation. The shaman can interrupt the manifestation with countermeasures and redirect the thoughts to healing, giving the soul tools to think "ease" instead of "dis-ease." Earlier in this book, I wrote that thought creates a vibration in the body, which in turn triggers a chemical response in the brain. That chemical reaction can be beneficial or non-beneficial. The body can react to those chemicals like an airplane in a tailspin; unless the pilot (soul) can pull out, the plane will crash. The pilot is in control of the airplane; the soul is in control of the body.

The Shaman's World

I walk between the worlds. I started in the lower world with the Shaman, in the world of power animals, quests, and journeywork. I then remembered my angel past and climbed to the angel realms. I left my connection to Mother Earth that I agreed to experience and sought to reconnect with the Source, Father Sky. I cannot forsake my Mother to cling to my Father. I must maintain a balance between the two. Mother Earth gave me the garden in which to experience life as a human, Father Sky teaches me the wonder of the cosmos. I am the connection of earth and sky. I am created in my Father's image. I am a creator and created the life my soul experiences. The earth is my base of operation, the school where my lessons are learned. The sky is the summit to which I climb; my Father waits for me there to show me creation.

This is the world of the shaman, the world between the spirit and the "quick" —the living physical. It is the shaman who rides the great drum to heaven and brings back the wandering soul of legend or myth. The drum beats with the cadence of the heart. The chant vibrates to part the veil between the worlds. The corn offering promotes goodwill from one seeking entreaty and beneficence from the spirits unseen. The graceful cacophony induces the disease to leave the stricken soul, to reassert a state of ease and fill the soul with love and trust, for the shaman has interceded on behalf of the afflicted. Balance is restored; the body once again operates from a center of authority.

The Native American form of government was a democracy with each tribal member given the right to speak with all the others listening. The chief was not a ruler with extra powers; he was simply the one who spoke for the tribe, bringing their words, and wishes together. The shaman, or wise healer, served as the tribe's spiritual advisor, holding the wisdom of the ages for cures, ceremonies and animal knowledge. He or she was the teacher, doctor, priest. Shamans were also isolated from the general population to maintain the spiritual connection, for the mundane rituals of the tribal life would have distracted them. The distance also allowed for spiritual connection by quest, meditation, and altered state. The brainwork needed for these activities was twenty to forty or more percent of capacity, and the need for concentration is obvious. The shaman had to live a life apart.

This apartness also adds to shaman's mystique, enhancing the power and reverence of that position. The power to heal comes from faith. A person's belief in the shaman's elevated connection with the spirit world helps the healing work to be effective. The shaman and I are no different than anyone else; we have simply maintained our connection to the spirit world.

My Quest

I asked for guidance last night. I put on a drumming tape and sought to go on a quest.

I am immediately confronted by a group of Native Americans. Gray Feather appears and introduces himself. He is dressed in a deerskin tunic of soft brown with fringes to his thighs; a kilt with fringes to his knees hangs below the tunic. His chest plate is decorated with intricate beadwork and around his head is a beaded band, holding feathers pointing both up and down. His gleaming black hair is pulled back into a long single braid. With him is Chief Joseph and two or three others unnamed. On my left is a figure I have seen before, the Falconer. This man wears dark vermilion robes to his feet over lighter undergarments. His headgear is black and white, with spotted tails of some sort. The robe is trimmed in contrasting beadwork and on his arm a bird is perched a falcon.

We are in a circle. They begin offering corn and squash, as well as turkey, and I see a deer carcass swinging from a pole slung between two trees. I ask, "What's with all this food?" They all start to laugh. Gray Feather asks me, "Do you know what day it is?" I reply: "Oh, gee. Tomorrow is Thanksgiving." I slap my forehead. We all have a good laugh about that.

The Falconer addresses me. "You are questioning if you have the expertise to express the Native American spirituality in your book. We have come to advise you. You have lived several lifetimes as a Native American. These memories are part of your soul knowledge. You have the information you need. We will help you access it."

I reply, "That sounds good now, but I need the words in the morning when I write my book."

"The words will come. We will guide you. Take heart," came his response.

And they did.

Chapter 11

Healing Codes
of the Universe

There are codes that have been hidden from the population since antiquity. Pythagoras adopted a mathematical code so powerful that he never allowed it to be written down. His initiates were sworn to secrecy, and the basis of his code has come to us only through dedicated research.

One test of Pythagoras' mysteries went like this: He would cause a great feast to be prepared, the table would be set, and all his followers would assume their places. They would contemplate the feast and visualize the taste, texture, and recompense what they would feel in consuming it. After a period of time, the feast would be withdrawn and given to the poor. The initiates would feel very satisfied, for in their minds, they had just enjoyed a wonderful feast. Their bodies were conditioned to release all the right digestive chemicals. This story may be a bit extreme. Raymond Grace, a dowser and healer from the Appalachian area, tells about his friend who lives only on water and peanuts. Voilà, the power of the mind.

Back to Pythagoras. He developed a skein of numbers that bears his name. The skein reduces all numbers to their bases and letters as well. It is laid out on the following pages.

The Pythagorean Skein

Even	Odd
$10 - 1 + 0 = 1$	$11 - 1 + 1 = 2$
$12 - 1 + 2 = 3$	$13 - 1 + 3 = 4$
$14 - 1 + 4 = 5$	$15 - 1 + 5 = 6$
$16 - 1 + 6 = 7$	$17 - 1 + 7 = 8$
$18 - 1 + 8 = 9$	$19 - 1 + 9 = 10 - 1 + 0 = 1$
$20 - 2 + 0 = 2$	$21 - 2 + 1 = 3$
$22 - 2 + 2 = 4$	$23 - 2 + 3 = 5$
$24 - 2 + 4 = 6$	$25 - 2 + 5 = 7$
$26 - 2 + 6 = 8$	$27 - 2 + 7 = 9$
$28 - 2 + 8 = 10 - 1 + 0 = 1$	$29 - 2 + 9 = 11 - 1 + 1 = 2$
$30 - 3 + 0 = 3$	$31 - 3 + 1 = 4$
$32 - 3 + 2 = 5$	$33 - 3 + 3 = 6$
$34 - 3 + 4 = 7$	$35 - 3 + 5 = 8$
$36 - 3 + 6 = 9$	$37 - 3 + 7 = 10 - 1 + 0 = 1$
$38 - 3 + 8 = 11 - 1 + 1 = 2$	$39 - 3 + 9 = 12 - 1 + 2 = 3$
$40 - 4 + 0 = 4$	$41 - 4 + 1 = 5$
$42 - 4 + 2 = 6$	$43 - 4 + 3 = 7$
$44 - 4 + 4 = 8$	$45 - 4 + 5 = 9$
$46 - 4 + 6 = 10 - 1 + 0 = 1$	$47 - 4 + 7 = 11 - 1 + 1 = 2$
$48 - 4 + 8 = 12 - 1 + 2 = 3$	$49 - 4 + 9 = 13 - 1 + 3 = 4$

The Alphabet in Numbers

A = 1	N = 14 = 1 + 4 = 5
B = 2	O = 15 = 1 + 5 = 6
C = 3	P = 16 = 1 + 6 = 7
D = 4	Q = 17 = 1 + 7 = 8
E = 5	R = 18 = 1 + 8 = 9
F = 6	S = 19 = 1 + 9 = 10 = 1 + 0 = 1
G = 7	T = 20 = 2 + 0 = 2
H = 8	U = 21 = 2 + 2 = 3
I = 9	V = 22 = 2 + 2 = 4
J = 10 = 1 + 0 = 1	W = 23 = 2 + 3 = 5
K = 11 = 1 + 1 = 2	X = 24 = 2 + 4 = 6

The next element in the healing codes is to assign numeric values to letters, as seen in the sequence on the following page. The table on the next page shows the interesting correlation between infinity and completion in the Pythagorean skein, whereby the number 9 represents completion and the number 8, infinity.

Healers through the ages have used this coded numerology to find the proper herbs and roots to effect good health. For instance, modern herbalists use it to correlate healing therapies by assigning a base number to a dis-ease:

Arthritis:

$$A = 1 \quad r = 9 \quad t = 2 \quad h = 8 \quad r = 9 \quad i = 9 \quad t = 2 \quad i = 9 \quad s = 1$$
$$= \quad 1 + 9 + 2 + 8 + 9 + 9 + 2 + 9 + 1 = 50 \ = 5$$

Multiples of eights	Reverse	Alphabet with #	Sum
1 x 8 = 8	8—Z	A—1	8 + 1 = 9
2 x 8 = 16 1 + 6 =	7—Y	B—2	7 + 2 = 9
3 x 8 = 24 2 + 4 =	6—X	C—3	6 + 3 = 9
4 x 8 =32 3 + 2 =	5—W	D—4	5 + 4 = 9
5 x 8 = 40 4 + 0 =	4—V	E—5	4 + 5 = 9
6 x 8 = 48 4 + 8 =12 1 + 2=	3—U	F—6	3 + 6 = 9
7 x 8 = 56 5 + 6 =11 1 + 1=	2—T	G—7	2 + 7 = 9
8 x 8 = 64 6 + 4 =10 1 + 0=	1—S	H—8	1 + 8 = 9
9 x 8 = 72 7 + 2 =	9—R	I—9 = 18 1 + 8 = 9	9 + 9 =
10 x 8 = 80 8 + 0 =	8—Q	J—10 1 + 0 = 1	8 + 1 = 9
11 x 8 = 88 8 + 8 = 16 1 + 6 =	7—P	K—11 1 + 1 =2	7 + 2 = 9
12 x 8 = 96 9 + 6 = 15 1 + 5=	6—0	L—12 1 + 2 = 3	6 + 3 = 9
13 x 8 = 104 1 + 0 + 4 =	5—N	M—13 1 + 3 = 4	5 + 4 = 9
14 x 8 = 112 1 + 1 + 2 =	4—M	N—14 1 + 4 = 5	4 + 5 = 9
15 x 8 = 120 1 + 2 + 0 =	3—L	O—15 1 + 5 = 6	3 + 6 = 9
16 x 8 = 128 1 + 2 + 8 = 1 + 1 =	2—K	P—16 1 + 6 = 7	2 + 7 = 9
17 x 8 = 136 1 + 3 + 6 = 1 + 0=	1—J	Q—17 1 + 7 = 8	1 + 8 = 9
18 x 8 = 144 1 + 4 + 4 =	9—I	R—18 1 + 8 = 9	9 + 9 =
19 x 8 = 152 1 + 5 + 2 =	8—H	S—19 1 + 9=10 = 1	8 + 1 = 9
20 x 8 = 160 1 + 6 + 0 =	7—G	T—20 2 + 0 = 2	7 + 2 = 9
21 x 8 = 168 1 + 6 + 8 =15 1 + 5 =	6—F	U—21 2 + 1 = 3	6 + 3 = 9
22 x 8 = 176 1 + 7 + 6 = 14 1 + 4 =	5—E	V—22 2 + 2 = 4	5 + 4 = 9
23 x 8 = 184 1 + 8 + 4 = 13 1 + 3 =	4—D	W—23 2 + 3 = 5	4 + 5 = 9
24 x 8 = 192 1 + 9 + 2 = 12 1 + 2 =	3—C	X—24 2 + 4 = 6	3 + 6 = 9
25 x 8 = 200 2 + 0 + 0 = 2 =	2—B	Y—25 2 + 5 = 7	2 + 7 = 9
26 x 8 = 208 2 + 0 + 8 = 10 = 1	1—A	Z—26 2 + 6 = 8	1 + 8 = 9

Table showing the correlation between multiples of 8, representing infinity, and the alphabet in reverse. When these numbers are added to the alphabet in its standard order, the numbers always equal "9," or completion.

Thus, the base for arthritis is 5. Corresponding herbs of the same base five are:

Apple: A = 1 p = 7 p = 7 l = 3 e = 5

= 1 + 7 + 7 + 3 + 5 = 23   2 + 3 = 5

Bark: B = 2 a = 1 r = 9 k = 2

= 2 + 1 + 9 + 2 = 14   1 + 4 = 5

Good Vibrations

I work with Solfeggio tuning forks. They are tuned to the original vibrations sung by chant and mantra in the early church. Over the centuries, these chants were corrupted by men of religion who believed them to be too powerful for man. On this note I will re-mind readers that the wall of Jericho was destroyed by the blast of trumpets; sounds vibrated the masonry and crumbled the mortar. Some very interesting experiments on sound or the vibration of sound (more clearly, sound waves) have shown that spoken words can evoke responses in water. Dr. Masaru Emoto's work with photographs in his lovely book, *The Hidden Messages of Water*, showed that the words "I hate you," spoken to water produce chaotic crystals, while the words "I love you" evoke an organized and lovely appearance. Sand, when spoken to in the old Hebrew language, will actually form the sign for each letter uttered. All these findings speak to the power of vibration and word is vibration.

The Solfeggio forks are tuned as follows:

1/Ut-	*queant laxis*	396 Hz $3 + 9 + 6 = 1 + 8 = 9$
2/Re-	*sonare fibris*	417 Hz $4 + 1 + 7 = 1 + 2 = 3$
3/Mi-	*ra gestorum*	528 Hz $5 + 2 + 8 = 1 + 5 = 6$
4/Fa-	*muli tuorum*	639 Hz $6 + 3 + 9 = 1 + 8 = 9$
5/Sol-	*ve polluti*	741 Hz $7 + 4 + 1 = 1 + 2 = 3$
6/La-	*biireatum*	852 Hz $8 + 5 + 2 = 1 + 5 = 6$

This may seem trivial to some, but the power of vibration created the Earth and can destroy it. One of the many reasons the scale was altered was to prevent Spirit from being transformed into matter. Heaven on Earth, that is how powerful these vibrations, can be if sung by the population at large. The Mi-528 Hz *ra gestorum* is the vibration used to repair DNA. Cluster water that has the hexagonal (six-sided) formation supports the matrix of healthy DNA. The chemical disruption of the hexagonal cluster of water occurs with aging and dis-ease. The cluster water hexagon vibrates harmonically with the Mi-528-Hz tone. The word "atonement" in the Bible may well refer to this characteristic. It doesn't mean atonement for sin; it means atonement with God, communication on the vibrational level in Godship, or, in more modern vernacular, to be "in tune" or "on the same wavelength" as God.

Plants and Herbs from the Bible ; Ancient Healing Codes

> *So eat always from the table of God: the fruit of the trees,*
> *the grain and grasses of the field, the milk of beasts, and the*
> *honey of bees. For everything beyond these is of Satan, and*
> *leads by the way of sins and of diseases unto death. But the*
> *foods which you eat from the abundant table of God give*

*strength and youth to your body, and you will never see
disease."*   —Translated from the Dead Sea Scrolls

Plants have been used throughout history, and even during pre-
historic times, by civilizations around the world for food, medicine, tools, household implements, and spiritual rituals. So it is
not surprising to discover that both the old and the new Testament
contain hundreds of descriptions of the use of herbs for all these
purposes. The following information was adopted from writings
and research by Terri Vandermark and Dr. Ellen Kamhi (see
"Resource" section at the end of the book).

Herbs are first mentioned in the Bible is in Genesis 1:29:
*. . . .And God said, "Behold, I have given you every herb bearing
seed, which is upon the face of all the earth, and every tree, in
which is the fruit of a tree yielding seed; to you it shall be for
meat."* Herbs were set apart from other forms of vegetation even
in the beginning. Another example of this is found in Genesis 2:5:
*"And every plant of the field, before it was in the earth, and every
herb of the field before it grew..."*

These two verses show that there was a definite distinction
made between the herbs and other plants of the fields. It is obvious that, according to the Bible, they were created to be distinc-
tive. So what herbs were mentioned specifically in the Bible?
Probably the most remembered are frankincense and myrrh, as
they were two of the gifts brought by the three wise men to the
baby Jesus—*and opening their treasures they presented to Him
gifts of gold, frankincense, and myrrh.* [Matthew 2:11]. Most of
the following translations were taken from the King James Version of the Bible. I have included here a wide range of plants and
herbs mentioned in the Bible, as well as their more modern uses
whenever possible.

Acacia wood is one of the first references to plants in the Bible. God instructs Moses to use acacia wood to build the Sacred Tabernacle and the Ark of the Covenant. Later in history, Christ's crown of thorns was also fashioned from the acacia: *You shall make upright frames of acacia wood for the tabernacle*....[Exodus 26:15]

The **almond** tree symbolizes many things to the ancient Israelites. An almond tree grew from Aaron's staff that his brother, Moses, stuck into the ground: ...*it put forth buds, produced blossoms, and bore ripe almonds*...[Numbers 17:8] Almonds have been prized for their oil and nutritive seeds in many areas of the world, and are an excellent high protein food, as well as being rich in minerals.

Aloes were used as an anointing balm for the dead, including Christ. ...*they took the body of Jesus and bound it in linen clothes with the spices (myrrh and aloes), as is the burial custom of the Jews.* [John 19: 39-40] Aloe is well known wherever it grows in the world as a healing agent, especially soothing to the skin. It is often referred to as "the burn plant."

Cedar: The Old Testament abounds with mention of herbs. Both aloe and cedar are singled out in Numbers 24:6: ...*like valleys that stretch out, like gardens beside the river, like aloes planted by the Lord, like cedars beside the waters.* The way **cedar** is mentioned in this context gives rise to the belief that it is the only tree descended from the Garden of Eden, as it is also referred to as "paradise wood." It is a very fragrant wood and the gum or perfume extracted from the wood was used for embalming dead bodies, as Jesus' was by Nicodemus:...*and Nicodemus came also, who had first come to Him by night;*

bringing a mixture of myrrh and aloes, about a hundred pounds of weight... [John 19:39] A prophecy about this was made in Psalm 45:8: *All thy garments are fragrant with myrrh, and aloes and cassia.*

Cinnamon was often used as a medicine, as well as a spice: *... I have perfumed my bed with myrrh, aloes and cinnamon..* [Proverbs 7:17-18] Cinnamon is a delicious spice long coveted for its aromatic qualities. Cinnamon was used in the holy oil used in the Tabernacle to anoint priests and sacred vessels, as mentioned in Exodus 30: 22-25.

Coriander also has numerous Old Testament references. The manna sent from heaven in the wilderness was compared to it in Exodus 16:31: *...And the house of Israel named it manna, and it was like coriander seed, white, and its taste was like wafers with honey.* Coriander was used medicinally and as a spice.

Cumin, mint, dill: Other herbs mentioned in the New Testament include cumin, mint, and dill (Matthew 23:3), where Jesus is quoted as saying: "Woe unto you. . . hypocrites. For you tithe mint and dill and cumin and have neglected the weightier provisions of the law: justice and mercy and faithfulness." The emphasis placed on these herbs in Jesus' rebuke shows their importance to the people of that time, for He wanted the populace to realize how much more important it was to offer up justice, mercy, and faithfulness.

The tithing of herbs dated back to Mosaic law, for in Deuteronomy 14:22, it was commanded: *You shall surely tithe all the produce from what you sow, which comes out of the field every year.* Mint was popular in Biblical times as a condiment and medicine, and grown throughout the Syrian region.

Dill is referred to as "anise" in some translations. It was also a popular kitchen herb at the time, and in the Talmud, paying tithes with dill required that the seeds, leaves, and the stems are to be used. Cumin was used in breads and stews and was also a popular herb for tithing.

Frankincense represents holiness, while myrrh (discussed below) is very aromatic and resinous and is obtained from thorn trees. Many believe the myrrh was to symbolize the suffering that would come to Jesus in the future, perhaps referring to the "crown of thorns" He would wear on the cross.

Gall is an herb whose name in Hebrew translates to "bitterness." It is mentioned several places in the Bible but most famously at the crucifixion of Jesus. At that time, it was mixed with wine and offered to those crucified to relieve pain. Gall is actually the juice of an opium plant and therefore used as a narcotic. *They gave Him wine to drink, mingled with gall; and after tasting it, He was not willing to drink.* [Matthew 27:34] The immediate reaction to that statement is that Jesus did not drink because of the taste, but further examination of the life of Christ shows that He refused in order to fully endure the cross.

Garlic was much prized by the Israelites. They complained of missing it after they left Egypt. *We remember the fish which we used to eat free in Egypt, the cucumbers, the melons and the leeks and the onions and the garlic.* [Numbers 11:5].

During the Middle Ages, it was a common Christian tradition to carry garlic as a good-luck charm that could ward off demons and vampires. Now scientific research has linked the consumption of garlic to various health benefits— including having the ability to kill pathogenic microorganisms. Perhaps their belief was not that far from the truth!

The **grapevine** is symbolized in many places throughout the bible. Here Christ states: *I am the true vine and my Father is the gardener.* . .[John 15:1-2] When Adam and Eve were in the Garden of Eden, Eve was tempted by the serpent to eat the fruit from the Tree of the Knowledge of Good and Evil. Although the fruit is not directly identified, there are many passages suggesting that it was the grape. Other fruits, including **orange, fig, and pomegranate** have also been considered. However, popular belief awards this dubious honor to the **apple**. The Apple of Eve represents the loss of innocence, indulgence and giving into temptation.

Hyssop is also referred to frequently in the Bible. It was known as a holy herb that was used to cleanse sacred places. ...And a clean person shall take hyssop and dip it in the water, and sprinkle it on the tent and on all the furnishings and on the persons who were there. [Numbers 19:18]. David also uses hyssop in a prayer of forgiveness. *Purify me with hyssop and I shall be clean; wash me, and I shall be whiter than snow.* [Psalm 51:7]

Mandrake: Throughout history, the mandrake plant has been associated with fertility and sexual prowess. It has a root that resembles a human image. Hebrews considered it a protection against evil spirits. Witches used the potent extract to induce hallucinations. Used incorrectly, toxins in the mandrake can cause dizziness, insanity, and even death. In the famous biblical love ballad, *The Song of Solomon*, there is a reference to the pleasant smell given off by the mandrake: *The mandrakes give a smell, and at our gates are all manner of pleasant fruits...*[Song of Solomon 7:12-13]

Mustard is another famous New Testament herb, mainly mentioned to note comparisons about size. *....for truly I say to you if you have faith as a mustard seed, you shall say to this mountain, 'Move from here to there' and it shall move, and nothing shall be impossible to you.* [Matthew 17:20].

Myrrh: In Matthew 2:11, myrrh is mentioned as one of the wise men's original gifts to the Christ Child. Myrrh is the gum resin exuded from a small shrub-like tree. It has been used to anoint the dead and acts medicinally as an expectorant or astringent. In the Book of Esther, there is a description of myrrh being used as part of the beauty treatment given to wives of the king:...*six months with oil of myrrh and six months with perfumes and cosmetics for women...*[Esther 2:12} In *The Song of Solomon* 1:13 and 4:6, myrrh is compared with the joys of sexual love.

Oak: In Genesis 18, the majestic oak tree is designated as the tree under which Abraham greeted two angels and supposedly God himself, all disguised as travelers. The oak is mentioned over sixty times in the Bible. Oak is important in all areas where is grows as a source of food, such as acorns, and for its wood and shade.

Olive: The following passage describes how to care for an olive tree: *Remember that it is not you that support the olive root, but the root that supports you...* [Romans 11:16-18] A branch of the olive tree was carried by a dove to Noah on

Mount Ararat, signaling the imminent recession of the flood waters. Individual olive trees can live over 1000 years, leading to the use of olive oil as a "longevity herb." There are olive trees in the Garden of Gethsemane in the Holy Land that are reputed to still be living since Christ slept there during His last night of freedom.

The **poplar tree** was used by Jacob in an interesting way, as described in Genesis 30:37-43. When his father-in-law promised him all the sheep and goats born with mottled and striped coats, Jacob cut poplar branches and arranged them in front of the animals in a crisscross pattern, while they were mating. An unusually high number of striped and mottled young were born that season!

Rue was used for medicine and in cooking, being very aromatic. Acting as a stimulant, it is also known as the "herb of grace." Brushes made from rue were once used to sprinkle holy water during mass. The version given in Luke 11:42 specifically mentions *...mint, rue and every kind of garden herb....*

Saffron: Along with other herbs and spices, saffron is mentioned in *Song of Solomon* 4:14, when Solomon is expressing his affection to his lover: *Nard and saffron, calamus and cinnamon, with all the trees of frankincense, myrrh and aloes, along with the finest spices. You are a garden spring,.* To be likened to herbs and spices at that time was a prized compliment.

Wormwood is often mentioned in instances where "intense bitterness" is the point trying to be made. *But in the end,* *she (an adulteress) is bitter as wormwood, sharp as a two-edged sword....* [Proverbs 5:4]. Southernwood, which is often grown today for its fragrant properties, is a species of wormwood.

Healing Codes Summarized

Given the popularity of herbs today, it is interesting to look at some of the oldest-recorded words in history and realize that, even thousands of years later, some things never change. The preceding entries emphasize that the Earth we dwell on can sustain us. The keys to that sustainability were written down. Knowledge was not for the elite but for everyone. Anyone can tap into the sacred geometry of the Pythagorean Skein. This mathematic skein unravels the mysteries understood by the secret societies and allows anyone to debunk the secrets. Remember, sound creates matter; we can sing down the walls of Jericho, China, or East Berlin. We are, each and every one of us, creators capable of Godship.

Book 2

Past Lives

The Station

I lived with my mother in a cage. I think I was the only child. I never saw any others. The station, the camp, whatever you want to call it, was a row of cages, each with straw at the bottom. The cages, about ten in the row that I saw, were square, maybe 12 x 12 feet. The bars went up and over the top. The door was at the front, opening onto a paved walkway. The separate cages were side by side, sharing one set of bars. Each cage contained a single female. The only redeeming feature of the station and the row of cages were the beautiful, tall trees that hugged the back of the row of cages. The trees offered shade from the hot sun. I never got outside the compound that I remember. The distant landscape appeared to be a desert, though with some sandstone outcroppings. In the distance, I could see some low hills.

I think there were males in similar cages, for I could sometimes hear them bellowing, but I never saw them. I think they were way down around the corner, maybe even at a different station. The females would get very anxious when the males bellowed, sometimes cowering against the back bars of the cage or grabbing the bars, swinging up and around, hanging from the overhead bars. They would charge the doors, but to no avail. Their actions scared me and I would hide behind my mother or curl into her lap.

All the females were young, with dark hair and golden skin. I thought they were beautiful. They had a language, using soft words to speak among themselves, which they did quite rarely. Their hair was combed with bones they fashioned, and sometimes, they would reach between the bars and comb one another's hair. The hair that loosened during the combing was so long they used it to fashion ornaments, like bracelets, necklaces, and even sleeping mats. Mostly, they were without clothes but when they could, they fashioned leaves to cover themselves.

Food was provided twice a day, set into each cage on trays by the keeper, whom I called "G-gar." He would let me help him, so he let me out of the cage. He had a wheeled cart I could push with the handle on the back, but when the cart was full and heavy, he had to help me until the load lightened and I could push it myself. He was nice and sometimes, he would tease me. He made words but I really didn't know what he meant. He did teach me some words. He made me a little tunic from one of his shirts. I think he was afraid I might catch cold.

I did see one of the women get sick. She would not eat, just lay on the straw. She didn't move for many days. The other women became anxious, screaming and crying, banging on the bars. I hide behind my mother. G-gar came and opened the sick woman's cage. He wrapped her in a cloth and set her in the wheel cart. I never saw her again. The other women had tears in their eyes for days. They extended their hands to the sky, slowly undulating and speaking softly in unison as the moon came out. Seven days in a row they repeated this ritual, washed in moonlight. I think I saw G-gar watching too, but it was dark. I couldn't be sure.

Early one morning G-gar came. I was still asleep. He grabbed me quickly from my mother, who tried to hold me back. He shook his head and raised his fingers to his lips. Mother went to the back of the cage and cried softly. G-gar took me to his house. He put me in what he called a "closet," way at the back of the dwelling. I could not believe what I saw. I registered all the sights, but had no time to understand what I saw. G-gar kissed my cheek and gave me a hug. Again he put his finger to his lips as he closed the two closet doors. I was in the dark. I trusted G-gar, I stayed quiet for what seemed like hours, sleeping and waking again. I felt of the textures around me.

Suddenly, I heard a very loud noise. It was not close by, but it shook the closet. I put a cloth over my head and shivered. Later, G-gar came to take me out. I wanted to go back to my mother. I pointed out the window. He shook his head. After that, he played with me for a long time and then put me on a pallet under the window. He gave me a figure that was twice the size of my hand. It had long, black hair and was soft, so that I could push my finger into its center. It had a face. I liked it. I hugged it close and fell asleep.

I sat up in the early light. I rubbed my eyes trying to remember where I was. G-gar appeared with food. I ate, and then he washed me in a tub. He smiled and played with my doll and me. I again pointed out the window. He shook his head, hugging me. He put me back in the closet, closing the doors. He didn't close the doors quite shut. I remained very still, but after a while, my curiosity got the better of me. I pushed one door open a crack, but saw no one. I slid out the crack in the door, and padding quietly on bare feet, I reached the pallet. I pulled myself onto the bed and stretched up to look out the window.

What I saw was amazing. G-gar stood on the walk talking to three beings. These creatures towered over G-gar. Their heads were reptilian, crocodile, with little round ears at the top of long snouts that narrowed down to a set of nostrils. Their skin looked scaly. I couldn't see tails. Frightened, I scampered back to my closet. I hugged my doll and didn't move.

Shortly after that, G-gar came to feed me and play with me. I was so glad to see him. I jumped into his arms and would not let go. He murmured words into my hair, hugging me, rocking me from side to side. When we turned to the window, I covered my eyes, becoming agitated. G-gar looked from the window to me and back again. He set me down and pointed to my eyes, and then to the window. I ran back to the closet. G-gar pulled me out again. He wanted me to tell him what I had seen. He sat me on the bed and knelt before me, so that we were eye to eye.

As well as I could, I described my exit from the closet. I made a picture with my hands of the three beings, with tall, ugly faces. I started to cry, but G-gar hugged me to him and wiped away my tears. I wanted my mother. G-gar shook his head. Again, I was tucked into the warm pallet with my doll. I slept. Visions of the strange beings tortured my dreams. I dared not cry out. They might eat me! I woke, bathed in sweat. Later that day, when G-gar came, I went willingly to the closet, hugging my doll. About mid-day, a loud noise again shook my closet, setting my teeth to chatter. Very soon thereafter, G-gar came. He washed me up and took me back to my mother.

Back at the cages, Mother had her arms open and I rushed into them. Something was wrong. I couldn't tell what at first. I pulled back, looking at her. She was dirty—no, filthy! Her hair was knotted with dirt and straw; her body was covered in caked mud. She looked awful. I turned questioningly to G-gar. He was laughing. I took my mother's hand and put it in G-gar's hand. To-gether I led them to the fountain near the house. Like G-gar had done to me in the tub, I washed my mother off. G-gar helped me. Soon my mother was clean again and I hugged her close. I no-ticed G-gar, too, hugged her and kissed her on the mouth. A very long kiss, I thought.

It was some time before I found other things had changed. Three of the cages were empty. The remaining women were very anxious, pacing, and briefly shaking the bars. There was a smell of fear in the air. G-gar did his best to return to a normal pattern. I helped him with the food cart. He would let me come and help him with other tasks as well, like fixing the food. I think he was keeping me away from the other women, for he didn't want them to frighten me.

G-gar wanted to teach me words and letters. We would always have to count plates, cups, and spoons. He made it a game. I loved him. Back in the cage with Mother, I would in turn teach Doll how to count, as well as letters, words, and actions—just the way G-gar had shown me. Mother was very interested in my playing and she would join in the game, too. I would praise her just like G-gar did with me. Sometimes I caught a glimpse of him as he watched us from the corner of the walk with a smile on his face.

I was seldom in the cage, for now G-gar took me with him much of the time. Mother, too, was in the house some of the time. She helped in the food preparation. She and G-gar would sleep together on the bed; I slept on the pallet. Mother would ask G-gar to let the other women out. He always shook his head. Life went on so and it was lovely. I was learning all kinds of things. G-gar made me books. He would draw pictures and put words under them. Mother learned too and was most pleased when G-gar praised her. He taught us songs to sing, silly little tunes. We worked and sang together. It was great fun.

One day, G-gar was upset. He took Mother back to the cage and me to the closet. I understood. They were coming back. I knew now that he didn't want anyone taking Mother or me away from him. The loud noise shook the house again. I stayed quiet. Soon a commotion was heard outside. I peeked out of the closet, snuck to the window, and looked out. This time, there were more of the beings. I counted 1, 2, 5, 10. I counted on my fingers and toes, and still there were more. They were so tall beside G-gar, I was afraid for him. Then I saw they had brought with them more women. The women were naked and had ropes around their necks; they were tied to one another in a line. Their hands, too, were wrapped in rope.

The beings were talking with G-gar, so the women crowded closer together, comforting one another. Some were crying, others screaming, and even in the house I could smell the fear. They moved out of range. I went to the closet and covered my face in my hands. After that, we didn't sing. Mother came into the house for good.

There were so many new women that some were placed two in a cage. G-gar had rigged up a wash area, and the women were taken, one at a time, and cleaned up. They groomed each other once they were back in the cages. Within a few days, their hair was shiny and their skin radiant. They began to settle in. Mother and I both helped with the food and the cart. The beings had left great stores of food for the camp, and as I passed, I created a lot of excitement with the newcomers. They would reach out through the bars and touch my hair, my face, and my body. I didn't mind. I showed them my doll. I even sang a little song; they would smile and try to sing along. Mother was sad about the newcomers. I'm not sure why. It was just that when she would look at them her face would change. G-gar was very busy. I would skip along beside him. I would chatter, or hum a little song. He was very preoccupied, but he indulged me.

I made little dolls for each of the women. They were very pleased, I think. They would hug them close and look at me, smiling. Mother was very pleased with me. G-gar, too, nodded, and smiled.

Mother was sick. She couldn't eat and her tummy was very big. She lay on the bed and writhed in pain. I could tell G-gar was worried. He tried to put cool clothes on her head, telling her to breathe and settle down. Blood came from between her legs. A ball the size of my doll came out. Still, the blood would not stop. Mother stopped moving around. She became very pale. Soon she breathed no more. G-gar lay down next to her, holding her to him. He kissed her face and hands. He cried. It made me cry, too. I just watched and hugged my doll. I didn't want to think about my mother.

That evening, G-gar took me to the women and placed me in one of the cages. I just sat in a corner; no one approached me. That night, at the full of the moon, the women began a ritual. I was drawn into the dance. I reached toward the moon. I almost saw my mother's spirit dip and flow as we moved gently back and forth in the moonlight. Then I understood what was happening; we were moving her spirit/soul to the next dimension. Her body appeared as a white vapor drifting overhead. The women rocked and moved her visage, pushing it gently upward on the air currents. I felt her kiss my cheek. It made me smile. G-gar also came and joined the dance. He took my hand. I looked up at him and asked if he could see her. He nodded and smiled down at me. For a week, we passed each night in dance, helping Mother's spirit travel to the moon, to peace. Each night her form would be less dense. The last night, barely a wisp was seen. We watched her drift higher, higher, and away. G-gar had tears streaming down his cheeks as his hands raised toward her. He looked at me and reached down to pick me up. He buried his head in my chest.

I missed my mother. G-gar did, too, I think. He seemed not to want me out of his sight. I would often think about the ritual we did, of Mother's spirit flowing in the air above us. It was nice to see her that way, so ethereal. At times, I was sure I felt her caress me. A warm flutter would surround my body. I could see a faint outline of her hovering. I smiled. I did my best to explain it to G-gar. I think he wanted to see her, too.

The station garden was located on the walkway across from the row of cages. One day, I was there picking herbs and roots for the meal, when I heard a noise. A being was striding down the walk, straight toward me. He was huge, dressed in a black leather tunic that hung to his knees. Fringe draped from the bottom of the tunic and from the sleeves, and black boots reached to his thighs. A short crop dangled from his right hand. He would slap his boot with the crop as he walked along. Each time the crop struck the boot, I would wince. My eyes slid up to the face. It appeared covered in scales; there were round ears on either side of the frontal lobe, its tapering snout ended in nostrils, and its mouth seemed to extend under the nostrils back toward the ears. I was too frightened to breathe. I stood still. His eyes were on the women in the cages. He never saw me. He continued down the walk. He stopped at each cage, assessing each of the women. I finally managed to slip to the ground. He turned abruptly and marched to the house. G-gar spotted him from the cook room and ran out, desperately searching around. The being shook his hand. I could not make out their words. I stayed put, willing myself to be invisible.

G-Gar and the being advanced to the line of cages. One of the women was selected. Her hands were tied and a rope was looped around her neck. She was led out of her cage by the being, but she tugged back on the rope. His crop arced at her legs and she jumped at the impact. Never having been treated so before, her whole body began to quake. G-gar implored the being to stop using the crop, attempting to explain to the being that the woman would be obedient to gentle treatment. The being only laughed, continuing to swing his crop and scaring the woman. I could see she was sweating and shook with each movement of the crop.

They moved away to the ship that rested some distance. away. Then they were gone. I stood up from my hiding place in the garden. G-gar came running to me. He scooped me up in his arms and ran with me to the house. He just hugged me to him and tears streamed down his face. I understood that he could not bear that I might have been seen by that monster. Taken like the woman, beaten with the crop. We were safe now.

That was my first lifetime on Planet Earth. G-gar was my twin flame. In the life I just described, he was my father. I realize I never told you what G-gar looked like. He towered over me, but I was only five or so. Mother was closer to his height. He was still more than a head taller then she. His frame was willowy, bending and moving with grace. His hands and legs were long and slender. His hair was the color of moonbeams dancing on the water. His eyes, like the biblical Noah, were electric blue. His face was open and kind, and I never saw him cross or angry. He wore a light tunic to his knees, and around his waist was a rope with tools attached. He usually wore sandals. He held no resemblance to the women. He was a creature apart. I never saw another like him. My hair, too, was light. And when I saw my face in water, my eyes were blue, too.

Egypt

This was a dream that appeared to me, lucid and repetitive, in my early life.

Aisha was an Egyptian princess, whose father was a pharaoh of a high rank. Aisha was forced to have a chaperon everywhere she went. She would one day be married to a complete stranger for the purpose of forming a great alliance for her family.

Being just so much property, that was a women's lot in those times. Aisha resented the treatment. Her guards were always deferential to her, but she chafed at the constant watching and following every time she moved. She was an only child and had been allowed to explore education, a gift afforded to few females of the time. Her parents indulged her interest in reading and studying. They provided a tutor and encouraged her exploration. She was also taught music, handiwork, the arts, and other pursuits usually afforded to females of the time. Her interest was hardly challenged by these elements, but she was deeply intrigued by science, astrology, history, and even mathematics. She was very good at languages like Greek, Latin, and Arabic, the classic languages of the times. These interests made it even harder for her to accept the fate she had been dealt. She longed to escape, if only for a time. Aisha's deepest desire was to be free, to be by herself and alone, just once in a while.

She would dream of ways to escape her guards. A couple of times she had actually managed to elude them, but never for very long. She was 15, almost 16, years old; soon there would be no escape for her. Time moved forward, sealing her future. Her father had already begun making arrangements for formal marriage offers. He had let it be known that she would soon be available to the right party. She strained at the bit to be free, if only for a day.

Then it happened! By chance, everything fell into place. She was planning to go to market and had made herself ready. At the last moment, her guards were called to help in another part of the palace. Quickly she made her break for freedom.

There she was, strolling down the street, heart soaring at the unexpected gift of solitude. Her step was light, almost skipping. She inhaled deeply of the clear air. Somehow it felt different, as if it belonged to her alone. The colors around her took on new luster. Aisha felt as if she were seeing everything for the first time. Deep in her reverie, she never noticed the large carriage that paced her, moving slowly along the street beside her. Suddenly, two burly men jumped out and grabbed her. One covered her mouth before she could scream in protest. They rolled her up in a carpet, lifting her bodily from the ground. Blackness invaded her mind.

Aisha clawed her way up from the oblivion that held her. She felt warm, almost too hot, as if she were in a womb or a bubble. Her mind cleared enough for her to be aware that she was in a steaming bath. Ladies-in-waiting attended her. Her first thought was that her father was preparing to marry her off to some stranger. The attendants realized she was coming around and quickly drugged her again, with a less potent drought this time. Though groggy and slow, Aisha was at least somewhat aware of what was happening to her. She was being dressed in fine, diaphanous garments. Her hair was already piled high with perfumed curls cascading down her shoulders, its raven hues accented with pearls. As she stood there like a living statue, the ladies covered her neck and arms in gold, highlighting the warm olive glow of her skin. On her fingers, gems in gold settings complimented her lovely hands. Her mind still in a fog; she could not fight what was being done.

At length, she was led to a high bed wrapped in veils and wonderful scents. The ladies departed, leaving her alone in this stunningly elegant room. She gazed around her in confusion. Unable to collect her thoughts, she was totally unaware of what was to happen.

A door opened. A tall man, broad shouldered and muscular, wearing princely garb and stature, entered. He greeted her in a language unknown to her. He climbed into bed beside her, reaching to caress her. Never having been with a man, and still groggy, Aisha pushed him away and scrambled out of reach, clutching the sheets around her. Startled, the prince tried to soothe her. She would have none of it, fighting him the more. He laughed and then looked more closely at her.

The prince jumped from the bed and summoned his servants. They conversed in quiet whispers, his eyes never leaving Aisha. His anger was evident. The original blackguards who had abducted Aisha appeared. He dragged the facts from them. He dismissed the perpetrators, uttering an angry oath at their retreating forms. He paced the room, running his hands through his silken hair, glancing at her wide-eyed form cowering on the corner of the bed. He moved toward the would-be bower and sat down.

The damage had been done; her reputation had been tainted by her presence in his palace. He could not return her to her family for she might well be killed. She was no longer suited for any kind of high marriage, and that had been her only value, he well knew. He called his most trusted servants, asking that discreet inquiry be made as to her family, he ordered that an offer of marriage be tendered immediately. He turned back to Aisha.

Well, well, well, he certainly had not expected this turn of events. He was an honorable man and saw no other option than to marry her himself. She was his responsibility now. How could he explain that she had been kidnapped and drugged by his people? A case of mistaken identity. Hardly! He was a high-born prince himself. He had no doubt that his offer of marriage would be welcomed, no questions asked. That was not the problem. He just didn't know her or have any idea what to expect. Not what he had planned at all.

What to do? Here he was with this wild, little kitten, cowering in the bed, ready to scratch his eyes out. The drug they had administered to her was still in her system. She was starting to shake all over. They had told him it was a strong aphrodisiac . Their plan to make him think she had come willing to his bed. He knew she was in agony. He knew not how to help her. Gently, he tried again to approach her, speaking soft soothing sounds, lightly running his hands over her extremities. Her dark eyes like saucers, she shrank away from his every touch. The shaking increased. Try as he might to control himself, her actions were stirring something primal in him. Cursing deep in his throat, like an animal, he drew her under him, pinning her flailing arms over her head. Deep he thrust into her, feeling the tear of skin fold. His lust out of control, he planted his seed almost at once. Aisha, too, was overcome by her deepest instincts and responded in kind, relief and surprise evident on her face. She looked up at him with fear and wonder mirrored in her dark orbs. That look would haunt him for years to come. For a while, she lay quietly under his body, his weight holding her there.

She rocked gently in a most sensuous way. His response was equal. His seed sprang forth. She answered in the most ancient of rituals. Time stopped. Each time, the call was answered. Their joining was cataclysmic. He was not without experience, but had never joined like this. They floated in space beyond time.

Hours later, she closed her eyes in sleep. He could not bring himself to leave her, with her heart beating like a tiny bird's, next to his ear. He stroked her beautiful, smooth body. Brushing her hair from her face, he gazed at her, taking in her form from top to bottom. The dark tresses of her hair. The warm glow of unblemished skin. Her face so innocent, lips puffed from loving. Her features were so perfect, he thought, as if painted by an artistic hand. The mounds of her breasts, nipples taut, begged his touch. Her satin skin was covered in a sheen of ardor, hips and legs splayed amid the sheets. In that moment, he vowed he would give her anything she desired. Kissing her cheek, he drew her closer to him, covering her protectively with his bronze arm. He closed his eyes in sleep.

Deep in exhausted sleep, he never felt her slip from under his arm. She pulled on the silken garb that had barely hidden her body the night before. The house was still. No one was about as she cautiously made her way to freedom. Her mind snapped and popped as ideas formed and flowed. Disconnected thoughts. Where to go? What to do? A plan! A plan! Think, think! She knew she needed a plan, if she was to travel alone, undetected. She knew she did not want to be kidnapped. What to do? Change her looks, become unremarkable.

Aisha moved quietly and quickly through the house. She located the kitchen. Taking a knife, she chopped at her hair. Hurrying, she left the tresses in a pile on the floor. Looking out the window she spied the laundry hanging on the line, including some boy's clothes. A plan began to form. Quickly, she ran into the garden and snatched the trousers and cotton over-garment from the line. As she washed the night from her body in a tub of cold water, her thoughts clarified. Once dry, she donned the clothes. With a knife and some food stuffed in her pockets, she was on her way out of the house.

Aisha knew she could not go home. All that freedom she had wished for, she now had. She hurried, running down the streets until she felt safely away. Finding a bench beside the road, she stopped to catch her wind. She noted the light was starting to breach the eastern sky. A noise insinuated itself into her head. Something was stirring, but her fuzzy mind could not put it together. Forms began passing by her as she sat. At first she panicked, but as her eyes became accustomed to the dawn light, she gradually she realized they were no threat to her. It was a caravan, gathering on the road to head out of the city. Perfect! The answer to her prayers. She slipped amid the flocks of sheep as they passed before her. Keeping her head down, she followed along, doing what she saw the other shepherds do. Her former life was slipping away behind her. All the protection and luxury known to her were but a distant memory.

The gods were kind to her. A merchant, who was the owner of the caravan, was a kindly family man. He was good to his animals and to those who worked with him. He had learned early that people who were treated with respect worked harder and took more care of his goods and his herds, which brought good money wherever his caravan entered a settlement. He had become very wealthy and happy, and was greatly respected by all who dealt with him.

Three weeks into the trip, the merchant noted a different face. He said nothing at first, but just kept an eye on the boy. Something didn't ring true. Aisha worked hard to fit in but the merchant was not fooled. He asked one of the shepherds to bring "him," the new boy, to his tent at the close of day, when the camp was set up. She followed the direction of her companion to the main tent. Heart pounding, she stepped inside. The interior was colorful, with carpets amassed and hand-crafted pillows of brilliant hues piled high. Here and there, small tables held beautiful artifacts. The merchant occupied a large cushioned seat as he pored over pages in a journal. His head came up He smiled at her and motioned to a seat near him. The merchant tried several languages before finding one they both knew. He spoke kindly to her, revealing to her that her disguise hadn't been successful with him.

With some prodding, he was able to elicit her story. He touched her pretty, soft cheek, looking at her lovely hands, and knew she told the truth. The merchant explained that the caravan would arrive, in three months' time, at the oasis that was his home. He went on to tell her about his wives and children who lived there. He assured her he would see her safely to his home. His wives, he noted, would welcome her warmly, and told Aisha that while she would have to earn her keep, she would not be mistreated. Once they arrived at the oasis, he would decide what was to be done with her. While on the road, however, he would apprentice her to the cook, conspiring with this same good person to see that no harm came to her. She was so grateful for his kind words, tears started behind her eyes. He kissed both her cheeks, patting her hands. She left the tent in the company of the cook. The merchant mused at the hard road she was likely to find ahead of her. He already suspected she was with child, for he had five wives and fifteen children to his credit and knew the signs. He would let her learn about that later, not wishing to add to her burden at this time.

True to the merchant's word, the caravan arrived at the oasis at the expected time. Amid the gleeful shouts of many children, Aisha was completely spellbound. Never had she imagined such a scene. Culture-shocked, she waited and watched. Aisha had been led to a bath area were she was able to relax as she washed away the dust of travel. She busied herself wandering around the oasis. The sights were so brilliant and bustling, she was entranced. Families crowded every doorway; children ran and played with abandon. She was sure she would get lost, so her walk was only within a very limited area where she could keep the main square in sight. Late in the evening she was summoned to the merchant's house.

The room was hung with beautiful tapestries, hand-crafted carpets of magnificent detail. Aisha thought that she had seen none finer in the palaces to which she was accustomed. The furniture was pillowed and inviting. Around the room were placed tasteful appointments to inspire warmth and comfort.

The merchant motioned her to him and spoke into the ear of a lovely woman next to him, dressed in robes of vermilion and yellow, woven in daring patterns and decorated with lovely bead work , who was sitting next to him. Apparently, the kind man had already passed on Aisha's story. The woman patted the pillow at her side, her long, heavy hair curling in little wisps that escaped the band that tried to tame it, as she made soothing noises in her throat. The merchant explained that this wife, Mira, was with child. He asked if Aisha would help her with the five children his wife had already borne, to ease her burden. Eagerly, Aisha agreed. She knew very little of babies, as he suspected, but both of them knew she would put her whole heart into the task, gratefully. She knew this man had, without a doubt, saved her life. She owed him her loyalty and would do her best to repay his kindness.

From that night on, life in the merchant's home settled into a routine. Household chores seemed endless. Aisha was determined to meet the challenge. She was assigned a lovely room next to Mira's. The room lacked the opulence with which she had grown up, but in truth, she liked this one better. Best of all, Aisha could come and go as she pleased. The merchant supplied her with garments and beautiful fabrics, from which she learned to craft her own amenities. She made hangings for the numerous tables and stands that adorned the room. She was taught to weave and produced colors and textures that pleased her very much. The room was becoming her personal oasis. These things she did in her spare time, after the little ones were fed, bathed, dressed, and cared for. She did love the children and they were very open and loving to her in return. This amazed her no end, for she had never experienced family life before. Mira was a wonderful teacher, imparting skills to Aisha she had never learned during her life as a princess. As the days progressed, she became more familiar with the dialect of the oasis as well, and felt a deep joy and contentment in her new life.

It was soon discovered that Aisha could read and write. Most writings of the time were done by scribes or priests using the classic languages that were Aisha's forte. People in the community would come to her for lessons. She would read their books or mail they had accumulated. Some documents were so worn the words were barely visible. Each was a precious family heirloom. She treated them with great respect, endearing her to all she served. Aisha also taught Mira to read and write.

It was Mira who gently prepared her with the knowledge of her condition. Aisha's body began to show signs of the activity within. Mira guided her with herbs and potions that were part of the ancient cultures of women the world over, balancing the flood of hormones and the body's reactions to the new life within, while explaining all that would happen and reassuring the girl that she would be fine. Having a child was a natural event. Children were seen as gifts of the gods in this culture, no matter how they were conceived. Aisha received only kindness and gentle treatment within the community, for which she was eternally grateful.

Two months after Aisha's arrival at the oasis and the merchant's home, Mira readied for her own lying-in. She asked that Aisha be with her during the birth. Labor started. The midwife was summoned and the other wives came to do their part. Aisha walked with her new friend, rubbing her back, holding cool cloths to her head, assisting with all the rituals that led to successful outcomes. The hours passed, the bed was prepared and soon the little life came forth. Such a miracle! Aisha, the princess, had never dreamt of such a thing. She was filled with wonder. Would she be able to do that when her time came?

The proud father arrived from his latest trek a week later to view his newest heir. Gifts were passed to all. Mira was declared a most wonderful wife. A place of high honor was made for her amidst the celebratory gathering. The merchant was a wise man and was able to make each of his five wives feel special in some way. Each was extolled with a talent that could not be done without. A wise man indeed!

Merrily dancing with each in turn, he grabbed Aisha, and, gently patting her tummy, he declared "And you, my dear, shall have two!" Aisha floated away as he reached for another partner. Turning to Mira, Aisha asked, "What did he mean, I would have two?" Mira patted the seat beside her, indicating to Aisha to sit, which the girl did. Mira said, "You will have twins, my dear. He always knows these things. Don't ask me how. He is always right."

Aisha asked in astonishment, "How did he know I was with child?"

Mira's simply repeated, "He knows."

The following day, when the turmoil of the arrival and the new child had settled, the merchant called for Aisha. He told her that he would be at home for two weeks and then would travel to Rome. She was to accompany him there. Her face dropped.

"Why must I go?" she asked. "I love it here and Mira needs me."

He hugged her, saying gently, "My child, you are a high-born princess, while we are simple folk. You must take your rightful place. I have found a family of your station in Rome. They have need of a teacher for their children. They are good people. I have told them you are widowed and with child. They are most anxious to offer you a place in their home. They will be able to introduce you to proper society. Someone of your station may wish to marry and accept your sons as heirs or, at least, as family."

"Sons?"

The merchant placed his fingers over his lips to silence her. He raised his hands as she made to protest. "Aisha, sweet child, I have been kind to you, have I not? You must trust my wisdom in this." Tears came to her eyes, but she bowed her head and agreed.

The weeks passed all too quickly. Goodbyes were hard, for she had come to love all the members of the merchant's family. She reminded herself that she was indeed a princess, and with head held high, she accepted her fate. Thankfully, the caravan departed at dawn, and only Mira was there to see her off. No words were spoken as Aisha climbed into the horse-drawn cart to which she had been assigned. Mira held her hand until she was beyond reach; then, with a gentle squeeze, the parting was made.

As Aisha joined the winding caravan once again, she was gripped with a sense of adventure. This time she was no shepherd, walking among the sheep. The small cart had a cloth covering to protect its contents from both sun and rain. The terrain they would cross was varied, some places flat and dry, others high and wet. The conveyance was piled with pillows and fabrics, as well as boxes of trade goods. One of the merchant's daughters, Sara, had come along to provide Aisha with companionship. Sara, who was perhaps eleven or twelve years of age, was all a-giggle at the prospect of such an adventure. It was a great honor to go with her father on caravan. The merchant thought it wise to have his daughter along for the journey, should Aisha run into problems en route to Rome. Aisha was well along in her pregnancy, and there was no telling what traveling in the caravan might do.

When the weather permitted and the land was accommodating, not too rocky or steep, the young ladies walked. The herds attached to the caravan moved at a slow pace, setting the speed at which the entourage moved. The merchant had learned early that hurrying was not profitable. The animals would drop weight, get sick, and be worthless. Aisha and Sara had no difficulty keeping up.

Aisha's hair was shoulder-length now, and she wore it piled high or braided to keep cool. Sara loved to brush it for her. In return, Aisha would help her with her letters. In the evenings, when the caravan stopped for the day, the young women would do needlework, making baby clothes.

The season was perfect and all went well for the travelers. The merchant plied his wares: at each town, oasis, or stop, some would be sold, some would be bought. The merchant was well known and well treated. His visits were times for celebration for the settlements. The merchant would set up a bazaar and the whole community for miles around would come. Each gathering had the air of a fair. The drivers of the caravan would use the time to practice their skills at wrestling and the locals would join in; prizes were given to the winners. Other skills were tested as well, such as throwing, arts, beadwork, and much more. The colors and horns would call the people to the caravan. Smiling children would hide behind the robes of their parents until wonder and curiosity drew them out to see the events.

The young ladies endured some interested looks because of their rare beauty and strangeness, as they were not the usual caravan attendees. Everyone in the caravan, particularly the drivers, were very protective of the young ladies and dealt quickly with any perceived disrespect.

Rome was reached in record time. The merchant asserted that the girls had brought good luck to him. It was their last night in camp, and the city could be seen in the distance from their position atop one of Rome's famous hills. Aisha's condition was really asserting itself. The next morning, the young ladies took particular care with their dress and hair. The caravan was left behind as Sara and Aisha journeyed with the merchant into the bustling city in their cart. Aisha had never seen anything like it before.

The gates of the city were ornate and imposing. Trumpets blared. It seemed that hundreds of people were all going to the same place all at once. Sara and Aisha turned from side to side, trying to see everything all around them. There were slaves up for sale and bidding was underway. Another merchant was hawking yards of fine cloth to anyone who would listen. Horses snorted and pranced in all the excitement. Sheep, pigs, cattle, ducks, and geese wandered everywhere. Caged birds squawked as they swung wildly from poles on the shoulders of their carriers. Too much to see, too much to hear.

The palace residence that was their destination was on a calm back street with large tree-lined walkways and peaceful fountains. It was warm and welcoming, and Aisha's new family-to-be seemed kind and happy to meet the young woman. They made Aisha feel very happy to be installed in her new residence. Even though she knew she would miss the kind merchant and his brood, as well as her companion Sara, Aisha knew that her future at the palace would be a good one. She was happy to be installed in her new residence. The merchant, with Sara in hand, slipped quietly away. He hoped that no one saw the tears that gathered behind his eyes as he bade farewell to the young girl who had become like a daughter to him. He was one of God's angels for sure. Aisha would not forget him.

During her first night in the palace, Aisha dreamed that someone had called her name. The dream was familiar to her, for she had had it many times at the oasis as well. The face she saw was blurred, but she knew it well, nevertheless.

Prince Galen had been searching the earth for her, ever since the moment he had awoken and found the bed they had shared empty. A search of the house had uncovered tresses of her raven hair. Galen had taken the bunches of curled locks and held them to his heart. The delicious hours might have been a dream had it not been for those curls. How could such a delicate little bird disappear so completely? In the excitement of the search, no one had thought of the clothes that had been on the line.

The prince wove the curls into a band He vowed that he would wear her hair near his heart until next they met. He sent searchers to every part of the city. Nothing! Then the search expanded to all the routes out of the city. Not a word. He raged! He stormed! He wept! He prayed! Weeks turned to months, months to a year. A lead here, a dead end there.

The night was Galen's friend. It was then that she would come into his dreams. He could hold her to him once again, stroke the lovely locks of her hair, peer deeply into her eyes as they searched his face in wonder. He conjured her form, lying beside him in the bed. He breathed her name, giving life to her being. He knew she lived beyond his reach. He had visited all manner of magicians and wise men, seeking word of her. Her escape had made her even more dear to him. He, with all his worldly power, had been given the slip by a young girl. He had to believe the gods were teasing him, punishing him for his ego.

There was no doubt that the one night they had spent together had changed his life. All the prince's affairs had been turned over to trusted lieutenants. He spent all his time and funds on locating her. She was his most important effort. One evening, a searcher brought the prince information about a caravan that passed through the city every year, and might have been there about the time that Aisha disappeared. The owner of the caravan, a well-known and much-respected merchant, must be found. Prince Galen prayed that in fact, she might have convinced the merchant to take her along. That might provide an explanation of how she managed to vanish so completely.

The prince had obtained the name of the merchant and learned about the caravan's expected routes, as well as the name of the oasis thought to be the merchant's home base. For the next month, the prince gathered twenty of his most trusted men and made preparations to travel there. Who knew how long they would be gone? Prince Galen pored over maps of limited accuracy to plot his route, for water and places to camp were a concern. He was headed into sparsely populated territory and areas not well known to him. Then everything was ready; departure was set for the morrow. His mind went through everything again; his heart prayed for success.

Dawn arrived. Prince Galen and his men set out of the city in high spirits, for they were all in the mood for adventure. Some might have called it "a wild goose chase," but no matter. Prince Galen was determined to find the home of the merchant. At best guess, it was to be at least a two-month journey. They were looking for the fabled "needle in a haystack."

The trade route offered easy passage, for it was well worn by the feet of centuries of camels, horses, and humans. After five weeks, their trail led them off into a more isolated landscape, one that had been less traveled. Throughout their journey, they questioned everyone they encountered as to the whereabouts of the merchant they sought. Whenever the prince's entourage stopped for rest and refreshment, information was high on the menu as well. Many to whom they talked knew of the merchant, for he had a reputation for fairness in his dealings and quality in his good. At first, those who were questioned did not want to reveal any information, concerned that he was being sought by a mounted company. Their fears were allayed when the story came out that the prince was seeking his lost love, and they became most willing to help.

After many days of riding, the oasis that served as the merchant's residence came into view. The riders had been traveling since early morning and were eager to rest. As they entered the oasis, a sea of urchin faces greeted them. Dismounting, the prince stepped to the well for water. Mira approached. Disdainfully, she looked him up and down. He sensed her hostility, but could not discern the reason. He offered payment for the water he and his riders used. She pushed his hand away. "You search for her," was all she said. His head shot back. He grabbed Mira's shoulders, peering into her face to detect any sign.

"Do you have word for me?" he cried in an anguished tone, and began to shake her. The children became alarmed, running away. One of his men approached and put a steadying hand on the prince's arm. Galen turned back to Mira. "Oh, Woman, tell me she is safe. Tell me she's alive. I beg you give me some word of comfort."

Mira took pity on him However, before she would give him the news he sought, she expressed her feelings. Any man, prince or scoundrel, who would resort to kidnapping and drugging a vulnerable young girl, no matter what her station in life, was not worthy of her aid. Galen listened with head in hand, nodding at her every word. The words were his own; he had told himself the same thing a thousand times. When her wrath was spent, he said, "I take full responsibility. I am the sinner. I should have protected any young woman's virtue. My punishment is deserved. I am not worthy of her. I have spent long years in hell, every day and night, with that same thought." He paused. Taking a deep breath, he continued, "Every day I have searched for her to put things right." Mira knew he spoke the truth. She relented.

Mira told the prince everything she could about Aisha. When she revealed to him that Aisha was carrying twin babes, he shot up from his seat and began to pace. Mira stopped speaking. He turned, "Did the birth go well? Where is she?" Mira told him that her husband, the merchant, had taken Aisha with him to Rome to a family he knew there.

"Rome? Why Rome?"

Mira explained that her husband knew many people. He was wise. He knew Aisha should be with her own kind, "...for the sake of the children."

"We all loved her; no one wanted her to go. My niece accompanied her. My husband will be here in a few weeks and he can tell you exactly where she is now living," Mira finished.

"Which way will he come? I'll meet him on the road," exclaimed the prince.

"I have no idea," Mira said, shrugging her shoulders. "Whatever way the wind blows."

Galen went to his troops, issuing orders. They would split up and head out in four directions. They were instructed to find the merchant get information about her residencem then they were to meet up in Rome. "I ride for Rome!" he cried. He would have left at once, but his men cautioned him against such haste. They and their mounts needed rest and fresh supplies. He was forced to spend a sleepless night. The dawn broke to his resetting the plan again. Swirls of dust attested to the speed of departure. Each band took their point. The prince and one other sped toward Rome.

"Foolish man," Mira thought, as she witnessed the exit, smiling and shaking her head. She turned back to her busy family. She pictured Prince Galen and Aisha to herself. Satisfied, she nodded and offered her prayer that the two would be reunited.

When Aisha came into the city and settled in with her new family, all her time and energy had revolved around the pending birth of her babes. The family protested her teaching the two sons and three daughters who were her charges, but she convinced them it would make the time go faster to be busy with the lessons and she endeared herself to the children at once. The physician and midwife, both familiar to the family, had found her delightfully charming, and visited regularly to ensure that everything was progressing properly. They had seen many births over the years, not all with happy outcomes.

One afternoon, as Aisha rested on the terrace overlooking the bustling streets below, a sharp pain coursed through her body. She knew her time was nigh, and asked one of the maids to fetch the doctor and midwife. Throughout the afternoon and evening, they worked together and just before dawn, Aisha was able to hold her two sons to her breast. Though she was exhausted, the joy on Aisha's face was captivating. The dark hair of the babes nestled in her arms was enough to bring tears to the hardened doctor's eyes. The midwife cooed. Aisha's adoptive family was thrilled.

Galen would have ridden day and night, but it was no small journey. His man held him in check. They made regular stops to eat and rest. Rome came to view after five weeks of steady travel. When he and his men had cleared the gates, Galen headed straight for the palace of his cousin. He knew full well no beautiful woman would have escaped his cousin's watchful eyes. His unexpected arrival would cause some raised brows. He was assured a welcome. He made some lame excuse for his presence, so precipitous was his arrival. The family seemed to accept it. No matter, his cousin was glad of the diversion.

After settling his man and himself in the palace, Galen was at last able to ferret out the information he sought. Galen phrased his words carefully, for he did not want his true desperation evident. "Well, Kinsman, how goes the conquest of Rome's true beauty?"

His cousin laughed heartily, "My dear Galen, I may have spared a few for you." The conversation revolved around a topic dear to his cousin's heart: beautiful women! Galen carefully said,

"I'm looking for one about 18, dark hair, flashing eyes, good dancer. Untainted by you. Any around like that? Surely in all of Rome, there must be one you have not managed to beguile."

His cousin replied, "I can think of a few," taking a sip of his drink.

"Do tell, Kinsman," he encouraged. Galen's heart was pounding so hard against his chest he was sure it could be heard.

"The sisters of Caligula come to mind. Silly, but very attractive! And what is the name of that young widow? She is stunning, a true beauty. I just met her at a recent party. Sad story. Two young sons, twins. Husband killed in the wars. Ah, but I think consoling her would be wonderfully rewarding. I may not wish to share that one."

Galen hid his excitement behind the edge of his silver cup. He rose and began pacing the marble floor, for he knew he had at last found his beloved. How to get the information he needed without tipping his hand?

"Well, Kinsman, it will be like old times! We'll wager which of us can win her!" Women and wagering were his cousin's strongest vices, Galen knew.

"Let the games began!" They clasped hands, pounded shoulders, and started making plans. Gradually, Galen was able to extract the news he needed. The cousin told him all he knew of the lovely widow: where she lived, her activities, her habits as he knew them, some particulars about the family with whom she now lived. He told Galen that she often went to a beautiful park along the river with the children, for he had seen her there himself.

Galen arose early the next morning. He hired an elegant carriage and six white horses, requesting that they be carefully groomed and ready by three that afternoon. He then went to the market and bought the most wonderful array of toys for his sons, who, he thought, must be around two years old by now. His face rivaled the sun in its brilliance. The shopkeepers noted he was surely a doting father. Getting help from the bystanders, he also picked out some suitable clothing for little boys. Once everything was packed, he searched for just the right gifts for his wife. Tears sprang to his eyes as he thought of her and his long search. He coughed to cover his emotion. He wanted to be very gentle, to show his love without making her fearful. A lovely tiara, sparkling with radiant jewels, caught his eye. He remembered her raven curls. Jewelry, perfume, pillows and fine silk, a special book of poetry, all wrapped in lovely paper. Satisfied that he had done his best, he returned to his cousin's palace. There, he bathed and dressed in his finest garb. The coach and six well-groomed, spotless horses arrived punctually at three. All the gifts were stowed away. Taking a deep breath, Galen directed the driver to the park.

Aisha, as was her custom, sat on a bench reading a book. The little boys played around her in the grass. The park was lush, with trees lining the perimeter. Paths crisscrossed the expanse of lawn. Statues, flowers, and fountains created nooks for private tête-à-têtes. The entire expanse was surrounded with a delicate wrought-iron fence. A motion drew her eyes to a beautiful carriage that had just pulled up to the gate. It was adorned with a regal crest and was drawn by six creamy-white horses. Striding across the park, a man scooped up one boy and then the other. Kissing them tenderly, he said "I'm your father. Come see what I have brought you, dear little ones." Totally surprised, they kissed him back. He turned as if to go, and then turned to Aisha, "Are you coming, dearest wife?" As if in a trance or dream, she obeyed.

Love Eternal

I told you we will lie in one another's arms
Me, 100 years, you 92, hairless or crowned in white
Together entwined our souls shall take hands
Follow the road to the other world
The Mirror World.
Our bodies discarded, our souls departed
Once in the light, Ah, the sight!
Forever young and free to love
Together we will frolic and play
Unfettered by bodies of clay
The Wheel of Life will turn
We may take up new form
Apart we may wander the Earth again
Always your soul and mine will find each other.
Time stops!
Your soul, my soul entwined, take hands
Follow the road to the other world,
The Mirror World
The Wheel of Life, Love Eternal.

The Lions

Carter and I once lived as lions, a past life brought back to my awareness when I shape-shifted in the "garden." When the intensity of the lioness came upon me, my persona changed. I saw with eyes of a lioness. I had the smelling acuity of a lioness. My perception was that of a lioness. Carter told me to make that change only in the "garden," for it was dangerous for both of us when I became a too aggressive "lioness" during love- making.

I decided to flex my shape-shifting muscle. "You want lioness, I'll give you lioness," I had said to him, and made the transition and instantly reconnected to my animal past. "Down, girl! Down, girl!" He soothed. It took a few minutes to transition back to human. Carter outlined the danger in what had happened. He explained that while I could make the shift in the "garden" with some safety because of the nonphysical reality, to do it on a physical level, in our accepted reality, was to assert wild animal intent. One would not enter a lion's den and make love to the creature in the limited state of physical reality unless one wanted to be mauled to death.

Rex was king of the pride. There were five breeding females and three young males still tied to their mothers' apron strings. I was heavy with a pending birth, my stomach dragging almost to the ground. I had given up hunting. Rex would bring me food after the hunt. He would watch as I devoured the meat, for he didn't want any of the others to steal it from me. Rex and I had been together a long time. He had lured me away from my family when I was of breeding age. Although he had taken other females, I was his first mate. I had birthed every year since our first joining. Some of our cubs had survived to adulthood; many had not.

Most of the time, our pride lived on a hill overlooking the great plain. The food supply was usually abundant, so we rarely had to relocate. Only when the weather changed and too little rain made the river dry up did we find it necessary to travel overland. We also followed the herds of deer, water buffalo, zebra, and other animals of the plains to ensure a good supply of food.

Ours was a strong pride, and very few animals would go up against us. We hunted as a team. We females would select a target, gather and walk casually around the herd until all of us were in our places. The herd would know we were there; they got tense and huddled together. That suited our needs just fine. We gradually closed the circle. The focus of each was intent upon our target. Closer, closer, closer, until the herd was densely packed, shivering, waiting, the smell of fear cloying the air. NOW! We would charge and the herd would disperse, leaving a lone animal, our target. We moved as one body. Rex would leap at the throat, while the rest of us jumped on the creature's back. It was over in a flash.

The herd regrouped and stood watching warily from a distance, counting themselves lucky not to have been the target this time. After the hunt, the pride moved in unison, dragging the carcass to the shade. The younger cubs and I joined the larger lions. Rex ate his fill. The rest of us relaxed, bringing down our collective heart rates after the fever of the hunt. One of the cubs approached the kill, disrespectful of its place in the "pecking order." Rex gave a warning growl, pausing in his meal. The cub beat a quick retreat behind his panting mother. Weaning cubs then took their turn, after Rex had moved into the shade to rest, digest, and standing guard while the rest of us ate.

The pride was satiated and slept in the warm sun. I tracked to the river. A long, cool drink was just what I wanted. I lay down in the cool mud at the edge of the water, panting deeply. Rex came up quietly beside me, nuzzling me and starting to lick my head. I rolled, exposing my belly to him, waving my feet in the air. I closed my eyes. His caresses felt so good. I was totally relaxed. Then his ears went up. Muscles rippled across my stomach. It was time; the interlude was over. I struggled to my feet. Rex remained where he was. He knew I would not want him to follow me. I slipped away to the nest I had prepared, deep in a cave. Away from the pride, away from Rex, on the far side of the hill.

My body began to ripple and contort, and my panting became more urgent. First, I circled round and round for hours. Then I dropped to the cool dirt. My body twisted, moving as if disconnecting from me. I rose up again, resuming my circle. My panting increased noticeably as the hours passed. Once again, I dropped to the floor. This time, I lay on my left side. I closed my eyes. Every muscle in my body was focused on giving birth. I began to bear down, and my babies moved down closer to the opening. I strained with a great effort. Relief! A tiny bundle slipped from between my thighs. Instantly, I rolled my head close, pulling the bundle within reach. I licked the sac away, revealing a tiny, helpless being. I licked and licked, moving it gently toward the underside of my belly. It blindly sucked, finally reaching its goal. The breath caught in my throat. Again, my body contorted. Another bundle slid out. I pulled it into reach and repeated the tearing and licking, moving my other tiny being toward my teats.

I was exhausted. I stopped for a minute to catch my breath. The two little cubs were noisily sucking. A third time the urge to push compelled me. The bundle slipped out. This time there was no joy! The bundle was a lifeless form that I pushed far from me. I would be content with the two I had. They were strong and healthy. I slept deeply for long hours. The cubs slept and sucked alternately, blindly bumping each other and me to hold their places.

By the second day, I was getting thirsty and hungry. I slipped from the cave as the cubs slept and trotted to the river. This was the most dangerous time for them, but I knew I needed to focus on my needs as well, though the well-being of my cubs was paramount. I didn't see Rex; he didn't try to stop me, but instead retraced my steps and stood watch near the cave. He kept his distance, for instinctively he knew I might panic if I smelled his presence near the cubs. Even he was my enemy now. I ate some grasses, caught a small rodent, and hurried back to my cubs. By the time I returned, Rex had vanished into the jungle.

The cubs were a week old before I left them in the cave alone again. Their eyes were almost open as they rolled and tumbled with one another. Already they would hiss and bat at each other in mock battle. I continually cleaned their little bodies, checking them, imprinting their scents on me and mine on them. My little male cubs were healthy and already weighed over ten pounds each. They would one day rule their separate prides, if the gods allowed. I knew their chances of survival were less than one in three.

The cubs, their eyes wide open now, were natural acrobatics. They would swing from my coat, wanting to play day and night. They kept me busy constantly, feeding them, keeping them in the cave. The two cubs ventured as far as the opening. A growl from me kept them there, no further. They sat on the dirt gazing out into the jungle. They were entranced with feel of warm sun on their fur. I needed to teach them safety, fighting skills, food capture, so one day, I led them out of the cave into the jungle, just a short sorite. They didn't want to return to the cave, so I would grab each one by the scruff and summarily deposit him back on the cave floor.

Their growling bellies brought them back to me. I dropped onto the dirt and stretched out, exposing my teats to their hungry mouths. We all drifted to sleep. When I woke, the cubs were sleeping, their breathing deep and sonorous. I took the moment to quickly slip out and pace down to the river. Then I took some time to find a meal; stealthily, I came upon some rabbits out of their warren. I dispatched them quickly and brought two back to the cave in my mouth. I returned to the sleeping cubs. When they awoke, I showed them the catch. They played with the young rabbits, interested. I then showed them how to rip the meat away from the bone. They watched and even grabbed at the second rabbit with their mouths and claws. They were fighting each other for the catch. They wore themselves out and came running back to me for supper.

As time progressed, my time away from the cubs could be longer. Before one of my forays, I checked the area. I thought I smelled Rex. I stopped and checked again, but nothing. Still, I was wary. I decided instead to take the cubs with me. This was their first trip so far from the cave. I made them follow me closely. Their interest in all they saw made for slow progress.

Halfway to the river they just sat down, too tired to go on. I rolled on my back in a secluded place. They drank, and then slept. I left them to slake my own thirst With a nervous feeling, I ran to the river, gulped some water, then rushed back to where I had left them. I scooped up one in my mouth and ran back to the cave. I returned for the other, running full-out for the cave. I was not ready for this yet. I tucked them in beside me, heaving a sigh. I really didn't want them out in the world just yet. Here in the cave, I felt safe, I could see them, and if I had to, I could fight off predators.

The cubs had doubled, tripled in size now. I had to spend more time away from the cave. Keeping the cubs full was taking all my time. They were eating fresh kill now. One night, as the cubs slept peacefully, I headed out, glancing around, sniffing the night scents, breathing in the tiny scent molecules floating in the air. Dawn would come soon and I must get back quickly. I loped to the bank. The water was cool; I walked in to my shoulders. The lap of wake made my fur sway. The water penetrated to my skin. It felt cool, Fresh, oh so good. I stood still; a fish brushed my leg. Quick! I snapped it into my mouth. A toss of my head and the fish was supper. That would take care of me; now what to feed the cubs? I watched the bank for some movement. A young doe and her fawn stepped meekly out of the shadows not ten feet away. I slowly moved closer, the doe's ears came up and she looked around warily. Her head dropped again taking a long drink. I pounced! The fawn was my focus. The doe bounded away., but the fawn, not knowing what was happening, hesitated for just an instant. That was the moment I needed. I took up the kill in my jaws and turned for the cave.

The kill dangled between my legs, slowing my pace. Morning light streaked the sky. I wanted to get to the cave so I made a direct line for home. The cubs would be awake soon and I needed to be there. Suddenly I saw him. Rex stood beside the path. I dropped the kill. Spinning away in a new direction, I looked to see if he followed me. He was. I drove deep into the jungle, taking paths away from the cubs. He followed. I varied my route. Still he followed. I was running now, trying desperately to lose him in the jungle. I plunged into the river far beyond the usual spot. I swam, jackknifing back on my earlier route. I could no longer see him, so I waited. Exhausted, I took some deep breaths and headed back to the cave. My teats were swollen and sore. I panted heavily. I threw myself onto the dirt inside the cave; the cubs protested their late meal. I let out a low growl as they latched on to me. They were getting strong teeth.

I glanced toward the opening of the cave. Rex stood motionless just inside. A large piece of meat, my kill, hung from his massive jaws. He edged closer. I couldn't move. He moved slowly, until he had the meat inches from my face. He dropped it there. He dropped to his belly; watching me and the cubs nursing. I reached for the meat. Rex slowly eased around to the other side, closer to the cubs. He licked my head, my neck, down my coat. Then he turned his attention to the cubs. Their bellies full and almost dragging on the floor, his sons looked interested in this newcomer. They sidled up to his huge front paws, fearless in their explorations. He allowed it. He even played gently with them. He licked the milk from their faces and explored their small bodies with great tenderness. I kept raising my head to watch him; he gave me reassuring purrs.

The cubs began to fight among themselves. Rex rose up and walked to the cave opening. He positioned himself to see all of us, the cubs and me, as well as to have a view of the expanse of jungle. He was on guard; I could rest.

Wagon Train

In the year 1772, my name was Abby. I had two older brothers, Joe and Davy, and two younger sisters, Em and Mary. My father and mother ran a little store at an army post in western New York. Mother worked in the store. I had care of the young ones and I did the washing, cleaning, and cooking. Most of the time I didn't mind the work. It made me feel very grown-up. I learned to read by pestering Father until he taught me. When mother needed rest, I even got to cipher in the store.

About once a year Father would take off with an Indian friend into the wilderness west of the Fort. He would be gone for what seemed an eternity. Mother and I were left to cope with the store, the children, and the house. Joe, the oldest, would pitch in. He was useless at numbers; however, he was strong and could handle the boxes, barrels, and stores. That is, when we could find him. He spent a good deal of the time getting into mischief with the other boys his age at the Fort. Davy tried to tag about his older brother, to Joe's dismay. They would end up pushing each other until someone bled. Brothers!

Father always had a high spirit about him when he returned from his adventures. He would swing mother around and promise to take her with him one day. He told of the wonders to be found around the bend in the river. He had seen great waters full of fish and high mountains that reached to the sky. He saw a waterfall that formed a half-circle of stone and dropped away to a roaring river that went on forever. He spoke of vast plains where the setting sun appeared to lie upon the land. We all sat, rapt in awe, at his words. He described herds of buffalo that stretched as far as the eye could see; and many elk, deer, and rabbits as big as dogs. Oh, he told great stories! The boys would beg to go with him. Mother's eyes shone, too.

Things were different on Father's latest return to the fort. Talk of rebellion was causing dissention and people were taking sides. The English soldiers were finding it harder and harder to keep the peace. I didn't really understand the politics at issue. I heard talk that people were sick of paying taxes to the king. They seemed to think they got nothing for the money they paid. The king was far away, across an ocean, and it was hard to be loyal to someone unknown and unseen. He only wanted more money and sent his soldiers to get it. Some insisted they needed the protection of the king, but most of these people had already challenged the wild elements, alone and unprotected. Our little store was a luxury many only experienced once a year or two, if not longer. They had carved a life out of the wilderness, without anyone's help but their own determination.

Father closeted with Mother upon his arrival. The next day, we all gathered to hear his words. Father wanted to take us with him; the whole family would go west. He said he didn't want to lose his sons to war. He didn't want to fight himself. There was so much beautiful country out there it was silly to fight. He would rather just move on. He said we would have to be self-sufficient. Everyone must pull together. We would sell out the store and take all we would need with us. He was not worried about food. There would be plenty of game, wild berries, and herbs. When we found the right spot we could plant seeds. The boys danced around, jumping up and down. The little girls hugged their dolls, looking a little anxious. I was ecstatic! Finally, I would see all the sights Father had talked about. Mother beamed at Father, for she had been waiting for this day, the day he would keep his promise to her.

The next months were exciting. Plans were laid out and lists were made. The store was the easiest part. Several buyers made offers. Father agreed to the best deal. Money was not really an issue. Where we were going money was worthless. He was thinking ahead to a time when others would move west or his children would choose to make their own way. That would be when money was needed.

Mother and I sewed warm clothes and packed away material, notions, shoes, hats, and yarn. Father bought two wagons. He would handle one and Joe would drive the other. They both had to practice with the teams. The horses and oxen were new to them. A four-horse hitch takes some getting used to. Mother and I practiced as well, wheedling the massive wad of heavy lines in each hand. The animals knew a lot more than we did. Maneuvering the huge wagons was cumbersome. The turns had to be executed at a wide angle to accommodate the team and the wagon. More than once, we got into a jackknife. The team would then have to be unhitched and the wagon turned manually to be hitched again. Naturally, we could not make these errors without an audience. Everyone but us seemed to know exactly what should be done. Thankfully, after much practice, we were all fairly proficient. The horses were very patient with us; I preferred them to the oxen. I named each one and made treats for them.

The oxen were Davy's pride and joy. For some reason, he and the animals had a special bond. He could make them do anything. This caused tension with Joe. Davy was to drive the oxen when we started out. It was clear to everyone that he was the better choice for the task. Father had to do some fancy footwork to smooth Joe's ruffled feathers. It was decided that Joe would lead off while the trail was open and easy to follow. He had a nice painted pony. He could really strut his stuff. That satisfied Joe. He would lead the little band out of the fort and everyone would see. His friends would be green with envy. So what if Davy got to drive the oxen? No one would see him way up on the seat of the wagon.

After four months of preparation, our family was ready to head out into the unknown. The wagons creaked under the load. Barrels of flour, sugar, cornmeal, and salt were lashed to the sides, as well as bucksaws and spare wheels. Inside the wagons, tools, cooking gear, supplies and food were packed in every available space. A goat, cow, and sheep followed in the entourage. We were not sure these animals would be able to tolerate the trail. If they didn't, they would serve as meat. If they did make it, they would provide wool, hide, milk, and meat as well. It was worth a try.

Joe on horseback led the way. Mother followed with the horses in the first wagon. Davy managed the oxen in the second wagon. The girls and I drove the animals with the help of a very smart dog, Rex. Father took the rear. He could keep his eye on everything from there. It was a lovely day and adventure was in the air. We all felt it. I turned and walked backwards, watching the safety of the fort receding behind us. Father came up and tweaked my hair. He didn't say a word; he just smiled.

The trail was wide at first. Our train moved easily along the route. We met some other travelers; they were usually men with hunting gear. Indians in leather and fringe, on lovely, colorful ponies walked with us for some miles. My family knew them; they traded at our store. They invited us to stop at their village and Father agreed. He wanted to trade for some of the beautiful, soft leather they were known for. My brothers and sisters were very excited to be going to a real Indian camp. We had been on the trail for a month. We were all in need of a break.

The village came into view. It was a cluster of square log dwellings on either side of a broad path. We stopped at a clearing nearby where we could move about easily. We unhitched the teams and set up our usual camp. Each of us had our job. I collected firewood, while Joe and Father went hunting with some of the Indians. Davy didn't like to hunt; he was in charge of finding water. Mother and the little girls cleaned and organized the camp. The Indian children stood shyly at the edge of our camp, watching all our activity. When things were in order, Mother told us we could run off and play with them. We swam in the river. It was really cold! Then we ran around playing hide-and-seek to warm up again. Davy joined a group of boys shooting arrows into a target. He was very accurate, and that impressed the youngsters. They made a headdress of feathers for him. He was very proud and ran to show Mother his prize. A girl of about my size took my hand and led me to her home. I met her grandmother, mother, and aunt. They gave me a beaded necklace entwined with feathers. They showed me how they had made it. I took a feather and some paint, drawing a picture on a leather scrap. They taught me some of their words. The time passed so quickly, I didn't want to leave.

Father and Joe returned with fresh game. Everyone had tales of the day to tell. Mother had made a large tub of bread. With that and some of the meat, we went to the Indian camp and shared our meal. The village was about 35 strong, young and old. After the meal, drums were brought out and a great fire was lit. The women danced to the drums. Mother and I were pulled into the circle.

The step was simple enough. I laughed and skipped to the beat. It was great fun! The necklace bounced up and down on my chest. My cheeks were flushed. An Indian boy jumped up and spun me around. Soon all the men joined in the dance except for the drummers. The children made their own circle. There is nothing so deep and vibrant as drums in the dark night. The moon was starting to show. The light of the fire seemed to reach out to it, inviting the moon to the dance. The parties at the fort were dull in comparison.

Father and Mother took the little ones back to our camp. Joe, Davy, and I got to stay. The drumming and dancing enveloped us into a trance. The boys joined some other young men. I was drawn to the fire. I felt a hand on my arm. An old woman beckoned me to follow her. I went with her to a small log home. The wonderful colors of feathers, woven blankets, beads, and gemstones decorated the interior. Three other women were inside. They signaled me to sit cross-legged on a mat. They began a ritual. One drummed softly, another shook a rattle, and two others swayed back and forth chanting. Wicks were lit. Honor was directed to the four corners. Tobacco was given in offering. The old woman told a long tale I could only guess at. I fell into a deep ecstasy. I don't really know what happened after that. Finally, I was led to the wagons. I fell into a deep sleep.

I woke the next morning full of excitement, remembering the adventures of the previous evening. I danced around during the morning chores, feeding the animals and gathering wood. After the morning meal, Father said we would take up the trail again the next morning. We were distressed to think of leaving our new friends. Father reminded us that we had much to do before winter set in. We had not even found a new home yet. The rest of the day was spent in preparations for the journey. Our new friends came to help. When all that could be done was done, Father released us. We skipped away, making up games and adventures to occupy the rest of the day into evening. We were trundled off to bed early that night.

Father had planned a trail of some 800 miles, more or less. It would take three months if all went well. He said there was a huge lake ahead, actually several. He felt we could find a perfect location to set up a farm in that region. He wanted all of us to help choose our home place.

With this goal in mind, we set our trail west. The Indians of the camp rode out with us. They were great company. They hunted during this time, and after a week they had all the game they could carry. We waved good-bye. They turned back east, and we continued westward.

It had been necessary to cross some very wide and deep rivers during our journey. The Indians helped us rig rafts to ferry the animals and stores across these places. It would take a day, or sometimes two to accomplish this feat. I wondered whether we could do this alone if we came to another such river. Father was reassuring. He thought we could manage since we had so much practice.

Some weeks after the departure of our friends, we came upon another wide expanse of river. We made camp for the day to assess how best to make the crossing. Father and Joe reconnoitered the bank. They checked for narrows and better banks that would make access easier. They swam their horses across, checking the depth of the water. They had not found anywhere to tie a line and rig a ferry that could be hauled hand over hand. That would have been the safest course. The narrowest spot was over a mile across and there was a strong current mid-stream. The plan was set upon to build a large raft. It would still take at least two trips to get everything across. The wagons were taken apart to reduce wind drag. The raft, with outriggers for balance, was constructed near the water. A rudder and pole were added, along with a shelter and some pens for the animals. Davy wanted a sail, and Father approved the idea. Five days of hard work rendered a marvelous craft. We christened it "The Ark" and were all very proud of it.

We fell asleep exhausted. Daybreak found us hurrying to eat, anxious to begin the adventure. Father and Joe would make the maiden voyage. They loaded one wagon and most of the small animals aboard. The oxen were lashed to the gunwale. They would swim across. The drag would keep the balance. Those of us left behind waved the party off. *The Ark* cleared the bank and headed away. The wind picked up. Davy cheered as Father raised the sail. We waited and watched as they floated out of sight, straining to see the speck slipping away downstream. We reckoned it would take most of the morning for them to make that crossing. Then they would disembark on the far shore. That might take another two hours or more. If it seemed wise, Joe would stay on the far side and only father would return. The west wind would be at his back, and thanks to Davy's sail and the lack of load, the trip would take half the time.

Mary was the first to spot *The Ark* on its return voyage. It was fairly skipping across the water. When he reached our shore, Father was exhausted. He lay on the grass while the rest of us loaded the last wagon onto *The Ark*. Mother and the girls settled under the shelter. Father and Davy lashed one horse to the rail. The others would follow. We took a quick look around to make sure we had everything. Father managed the sail, Davy the rudder, and I pushed off with the pole. We cleared the bank and headed into the river. The horses walked, and then swam along in the wake. We hit the current. Without the drag of the oxen, *The Ark* was spun into the current. I was standing at the rail, watching the bank recede, when a sudden jolt knocked me off my feet and overboard, into the river. I went down, down, down. The rest of the family never saw what happened. They were too busy fighting the current to stay on course.

I was a good swimmer. I loved the water and wasn't afraid. I was sure I could get back to *The Ark*. I kicked off my shoes, and struggled out of my overclothes. All the while, the current dragged me down the river, away from *The Ark*, away from my family. When I realized I was too far away with no hope of reaching my goal, I started to flag. Exhaustion was gripping me. A small log drifted within reach. I snagged it and just hung on. Floating along in the current, mile after mile slipped away. Finally, the current pushed me to one bank where rugged rocks caught the flow and slowed the current. I broke free and paddled to shore. The bank was steep here. I dug my fingers into the mud and hauled myself up grabbing limbs and bushes. I reached the top and flung myself onto the grass, breathing hard. I was covered in caked mud and sweat. I felt like a freshly-caught fish just off the hook, flopping on the ground, mouth open, gulping air. I fell asleep just where I lay. The warm sun of high summer blanketed me. When I awoke, it was twilight. I had had enough water for a while, but food was strong on my mind.

I picked myself up and scanned the surrounding landscape. Grasslands, low bushes, and some trees met my gaze. I wanted to clean off the mud and sweat from my body. It was sun-dried and seemed to be shrinking on my skin. I took some sweet grass, making a bunch in my hand that I then rubbed over my skin. It was moist enough to absorb some of the mud cakes. I walked along as I worked on my skin. I came across a small stream that rushed into the great river. With no clear plan, I followed it westward. The setting sun left a trace of color to guide me. I walked until it was too dark to see. I curled up in the tall grasses, and fell asleep to the soft gurgle of the nearby stream.

The sun warmed my face. I awoke, expecting to see my family. Then I remembered. I cried, head in hands. That made me feel better, but it hardly solved my dilemma. I washed in the stream and had a drink of clear water. In my hunger, I chewed some tough grasses that grew along the stream. Then I headed west again, keeping the sun at my back. I had to think that I might find my family. They were headed west, so I would head west.

I was too young to think that I might die in this vast land, alone. I walked briskly along, humming, continuing until I tired. I sat down to rest, and fell asleep in the sweet grass again. The night had crept up as I slept.

I awoke in darkness. Sitting up, I saw a strange glow in the distance. I thought to investigate and cautiously headed toward it. There was enough light from the glow so that I didn't stumble. The scene was riveting. There was a campfire overhung with a tripod. The scent of venison wafted on the air. Drawing closer, I spied the figure of a young man standing before the fire: a beautiful, bronzed Indian. I stopped in my tracks and dropped to my knees. I didn't think he saw me. I didn't know what to do. My stomach growled; the scent of the meat was tantalizing all my senses. My eyes were riveted to the fire. Suddenly, the grass beside me rustled as if brushed by the wind. I turned and saw that bronzed body standing over me.

I was dumbstruck. The Indian looked me up and down, and then he smiled and reached out his hand. I took it. He led me to the fire. He bent to the spitting meat and handed some to me, signaling that it was hot. I found a broad leaf to accept the offering. He nodded approvingly. I brought the meat to my nose, inhaling the aroma deeply with my head tipped back. My Bronze was laughing at me. I tossed my head and blew the meat cool. He added a small root to my leaf plate. I offered a few berries I had picked on the trail. He produced a bladder of ginger water to share. The meal finished, he tried to ask me how I came to arrive at his camp. His words were unknown to me, but his hand signals were clear enough. I pantomimed driving west in the wagon with my family, falling into the river and walking westward.I believe he got the idea.

My undergarments were torn and flimsy; they barely covered my body. My Bronze took a deer skin out of his pack. He put it up to my frame and made some marks. With bone and sinew, he quickly made up a shift. I slipped it over my head. It fell from my shoulders to my knees with fringe at the armholes and bottom. It was soft and wonderful. I danced around the fire with my arms in the air, smiling and laughing. My Bronze sat watching, and then he stepped up to me. I stopped. He reached out and took me in his arms. He rubbed my nose and kissed my lips. That had never happened to me before! He let me go. I brought my hand to my lips, looking at him in astonishment. He tossed his head and danced me around the fire, breaking into a throaty chant. We continued until we were both dizzy and exhausted. We collapsed on the ground and fell asleep nestled in each other's arms.

I awoke with warm, wet ooze between my legs. Oh, no! My woman time. At home, Mother and I had a supply of cloths. What could I do in the middle of this vast land? I headed for the stream that I had been following. I washed myself off. I still had the undergarments that survived my trip down the river. I began tearing these in strips. I was so intent on my work, I didn't hear my Bronze approach. I was startled when I felt his light touch on my shoulder. He knelt down beside me. He could see my legs were covered in blood. He hugged me and smiled. He then made a block of dry dirt patting it very thinly. He covered it with grass and wrapped the whole thing in a piece of the cloth I had ripped. He tied strings of deer hide on the ends, and then he slipped it under my shift and tied it around my waist. We washed me clean of the oozing blood. The rest of the flow was caught in the diaper he had made. We made some more blocks and wrapped them. All I had to do was replace the blocks when they became saturated. We held hands, walking back to camp.

My Bronze took some eggs and meat and cooked them on a hot rock in the fire. We ate. He tried with gestures and words to tell me of his mission. Somehow, I understood what he was sharing. He had come on a quest. He prayed his spirit guides would help him make a great decision. He must take a wife, yet he could not choose the one that would be his special woman, his life mate. He had been praying for guidance when he saw the shine of my eyes as I crouched outside his firelight. My face had appeared to him in the smoke of the fire. He took that as a sign. He believed it was I whom the spirit guides wished him to share his life with. He would be blessed by the "White Buffalo Woman."

I was amazed by his story. I, too, had been praying. Not for a mate exactly, but for someone to be with in all this vast loneliness. He pulled me close to him. He began a chant that was a prayer and he encouraged me to join in. He picked up a drum and handed me a rattle. We danced around absorbed in the sound. A gentle wind arose, swirling around us, kissing our cheeks. My Bronze's eyes got very bright. I could not refuse such a proposal.

My Bronze and I stayed at the camp for some days. He explained that his name was "Little Deer Hunter." His father, "Deer Hunter," was an elder of their tribe. A second elder, in fact, meaning that if the first elder were hurt or killed, he would ascend to chief elder. Little Deer Hunter himself was in the line of succession, for the present chief elder had lost both of his sons. Bronze's people were known as the Deer People. While he was talking, a large bird circled overhead close to the earth. He said it was one of his spirit guides, Eagle. My "Bronze" said I could call him that; it would be our special name. He would call me "Flower from the Water," since it was the river that had delivered me to him. He told me it would be a year or more before we could have the ceremony of union. During that time, he would have to prove himself worthy of providing home and hearth to me. Rituals would be conducted to insure a fertile and healthy outcome. I also would have much to do in preparation. I would need to fit out my new home and sew proper costumes. My Bronze said he would give me into his grandmother's capable hands. He made me feel so warm, and cherished, and safe. I spoke of my family. I started to cry, and he held me in his arms, kissing away my tears. When I asked if he thought I might see them again, he replied without hesitation, "If not in this world, then the next." His words were so sure. My heart was his.

We broke camp. He put me on his horse, a lovely black, brown and white pinto. We headed into the west, toward the distant mountains. We traveled six days. Each night we made a travel camp and ate food we had caught during the day. The last day, we topped a rocky ridge. The valley revealed on the far side was dotted with strange tents. "Tepees," Bronze called them. Tall tripods of wood reached skyward covered with leather stretched tight over the frames. Colorful designs decorated the surfaces. Dispersed among the tepees, men, women and children were all busy at various chores, moving gracefully. Horses grazed in groups. The scene was thrilling. Bronze let out a wild yelp. All eyes shifted in our direction. Some of the men caught up horses and swung toward us, racing at incredible speed. They were whooping, waving and yelping. They clapped Bronze on the shoulders and back. My presence seemed to puzzle them. They looked from Bronze to me and back again. They became subdued and we moved forward. Our welcome committee filed out behind us. So it was we entered the village.

Bronze gave me into the hands of his mother and grand-mother. Before he let me go, he explained that he would request a counsel this evening. He would make his formal appeal for marriage, introduce me and tell of our meeting. The women lead me to a tepee, smiling and chattering. They turned me, measured me, and patted me. I was led to a quiet pond and helped to bathe. They washed and plaited my hair, marveling at the blond color. My blue eyes also interested them. They treated me like a princess. They indicated I should then rest.

As I drifted to sleep, I watched as they busied themselves cutting and sewing. I think other women slipped in and out while I slept. I awoke feeling rested. It took a minute for me to focus on where I was. Wonderful smells wafted to me from somewhere. The clamor of the village existed just beyond my awareness. My eyes adjusted to the light. Little faces peeked in at me from the doorway. I stirred, giggles erupted, and the little faces disappeared.

I sat up and stretched, and yawning, took in my surroundings. A jar of water was placed nearby. I splashed my face. I stood. Beside me lay a beautiful buckskin garment. It was white with long fringe at the bottom and sleeves. Beads decorated the bodice spilling down the entire front mingling with fringe at the bottom. I was marveling at its details when the mother and grandmother appeared. They were delighted to see me admiring the dress. They gestured for me to put it on. I reached out and hugged them. I held the dress to me and danced around. We all laughed. They helped me raise the dress over my head. It fit like a glove. They were aglow with pride. Solemnly, they presented me with matching armbands, a headdress with feathers dangling at the ears, and last, but not least a pair of white moccasins. These were so soft, not like the stiff boots I knew. I kissed each of their dear faces. I thought: this is my new family. How lucky I am to have been blessed with two wonderful families in a lifetime.

I was given a light meal. The festivities later would include a feast. From their gestures, I took it to be a big feast. They rubbed their stomachs and puffed their cheeks. They led me out into the late afternoon. The little faces I had seen were attached to six little girls, who stood now in awe. Their eyes were so shiny and bright. I took the nearest hands and the girls formed a line on either side of me. So we came to the main concourse. Bronze stood to one side flanked by men of the tribe. I stopped short; he had my heart. He stood tall; a headdress of feather and bead accented his height. His skin shone like a new penny. The leather vest he usually wore was replaced with a collar of intricate design woven with coins, beads, and feathers, reaching to his midriff. His loins were covered in a dark, reddish leather, fringed at the bottom. His strong legs were revealed. On his feet leather boots reached to his knees, beaded and fringed. He was a beautiful Adonis. He took my breath away. I must have had the same effect on him. We stood transfixed, until little giggles broke the moment.

The women hurried me away, talking, tittering, and taking side-glances at me. All the women and girls of the camp were gathered together. I was introduced as Flower of the Water. I was hugged and made welcome. Flanked by Mother and Grandmother, a line was formed. Each woman and girl was introduced in turn, and a kiss or hug exchanged. I was given gifts: beads, colored bowls, jars, moccasins, woven mats, and tools. Mother and Grandmother took note of each gift and the giver. I was overwhelmed. These were precious things. The line ended and I was surrounded by the gifts. I stepped out. I honored each of the women and girls with a bow and thank you. I hugged as many as I could, trying to put name to face. Giggles greeted my errors.

Grandmother invoked a prayer to which all chanted. I heard "White Buffalo Woman" intoned. It was a prayer of blessing on the tribe, and on the new union that was about to be announced. That it would be a fruitful union, blessed with many offspring. And a happy union, with long days. The ceremony ended. A great shout was heard from the concourse.

A huge fire lit up the center of the village. The men were assembling drums, rattles, and chimes. Children danced around wildly, chanting, laughing and squealing. The women stood on one side, the men on the other. When everything was ready a tall man in a headdress stood up. Even the children hushed. He called a circle, invoked the directions, and invited the Great Spirit, the Ancestors, and the Guides to honor us with their presence. A great honor had been bestowed on this tribe. The celebration was dedicated to all the great ones that had a hand in the events that this and many blessings may come to the Deer People. A chant was then intoned. Bronze stood before the Chief Elder.

"I come before you to propose a union between myself and Flower of the Water," he said. He turned and made his plea to all. He told how he had gone on quest to ask his guides for direction in the choice of a wife. He had built a fire and was seeking his guides. A face appeared to him. There was silence as Bronze spoke: "I opened my eyes and there in the firelight was the face of my vision." He turned to me and took my hand, drawing me with him. We stood before the chief. "I ask for our union already blessed by the Holy Ones," said Bronze. Pandemonium broke out: cheering, hooting, and clapping. The chief called for order. He took our hands and placed them together in his. To each of us he said, "This is a soul oath." He went on to explain the requirements that must be met, giving each of us our roles in the pact. Bronze was to provide home, food, and goods. I was to make the garments and housewares needed for our new separate household. He said that when the requirements were met, a date would be set for the union.

The chief then addressed the tribe. "This union is a blessing for all. We will endeavor to assist Little Deer Hunter and Flower of the Water in their union." The formal rite over, the feast began. Bronze took me behind a tepee. He held me close, kissing me tenderly. A yelp interrupted the interlude. We were dragged apart. It was clear we would have no privacy. The dancing and eating seemed to go on forever: a full three days, I think. I began to realize how truly important our union was.

The next morning, the holy man selected and consecrated the spot that would be our home. Bronze had been given the poles and skin to build a tepee. I watched in fascination as the structure was raised. Bronze and I were allowed to be together, but always under the eyes of an elder man or woman. Bronze stayed in the new home, while I was housed with Mother and Grandmother.

I was taught the work of the women of the tribe. I learned crafts, beading, tanning, cooking, and painting. I was instructed in the sacred ceremonies. I learned to take down a tepee, and make a travois with the poles. The tribe wintered in the mountains. The plain became too full of snow to move easily. There were caves in the mountains and the trees diverted some of the snow. By late autumn the village was packed up and the long trek to the mountains began. Snow was on the earth when we reached the winter camp. Food stores were placed in icehouses and guarded continuously against marauding animals. Heavy buffalo robes were added to the walls of the tepees. Wood was collected. The Great Spirits were asked to bless the tribe during the winter. I was kept busy sewing my wedding dress. I had to create my garments and crafts to express my desire for the success of our union. The symbols on my items, like a family crest, bespoke of our dreams and the spirits of protection for husband and children. These would define our family to the tribe.

Sometimes I would think of my first family, wondering if they had found their place. I said prayers for their safety. I prayed that we would be reunited in this world, or the next, just as Bronze had said.

During my free time, I would teach the children to count and how to write down the numerals. The children would show their family. One day the chief paid a visit. He asked about the things I was teaching. I told him my father had run a store and I helped him. I had learned to calculate how much food a trapper would need to take with him to survive in the wilderness until he could return again for more supplies. I demonstrated to the chief using a piece of hide on which to make the calculations. He was very impressed. I showed how much food the tribe would need to get past the winter. Of course, he knew this by practice. He was amazed to see it written down. This led to my being deemed a Wise Woman, affirming their belief that the Great Spirits had indeed sent me to bless their tribe.

Spring came. The trek to our summer home was made. Bronze again requested counsel. Our preparations were inspected. The time for our union was set for two moons hence. I was so excited I could barely contain myself. During this period the women taught me my part in the ritual. I practiced it over and over again. I was sure I would forget something. Grandmother sat me down and explained each part and what it meant. After that it flowed very naturally. I thought of the meaning that I was expressing with each move, chant, or word.

Indians from other tribes began to appear three days before the event. The number swelled to over two hundred that I could count. Before this, it had not even occurred to me that other tribes existed. The import of the ceremony was impressed upon me. I was introduced to so many guests that I couldn't begin to remember their names. Hunting parties were arranged, and games for the children. The women cooked. I was not allowed to work; my job was to socialize. I found two white hunters attached to one of the Indian groups. Their eyes betrayed surprise at seeing me. I was dressed in the garment made by my new mother and grandmother. Those two women escorted me everywhere. The hunters bowed respectfully. They asked politely how I came to be here. I told them. They recounted tales they had heard of the Wise Woman sent to the tribe by the Great Spirit. When offered the opportunity to attend the union, they accepted. They also knew of the fort and the story of my first father's plan to go west. I asked that if by some chance they caught up with my family, to tell them I was well and very happy and wished the same for them.

At last the time came. It was late afternoon of a midsummer day. The ritual began with each of the visiting parties bringing offerings. They were introduced formally to the elders, and to the bride surrounded by the women, and the groom with the men. Thank goodness Bronze and I were seated, as well as the chief. The others could come and go, as they needed. The holy man opened the ritual. He called upon the spirits, ancestors, and totems to give blessing. He rattled and drummed around the whole arena. Little girls danced around tossing flower petals. Young boys carried smudge pots. These were followed by older youths, colorfully dressed, weaving in and out. The ceremonial fire was lit. A hush fell among the crowd. Bronze stepped forward, taking my hand. He presented me to the assembly. Then to the chief the solemn words were spoken. The ritual unraveled in a deeply moving progression. Every word and deed expressed my true feelings. Bronze looked so deep into my eyes, I melted. The union was made. No one could separate us now!

Then the feast began. Twilight was falling. The drums were at fever pitch. Everyone was dancing, chanting, and toasting the union. Bronze spirited me away to our home. He caressed me and the moment lingered. He slipped off my dress, and I helped remove his garments and footwear. We lay down on a warm, soft pallet. We lay there, exploring each other until the moment came. He entered gently, then urgently. Time stopped; we floated away among the stars. The angels wrapped us in their wings.

We lay sated, unable to disentangle, and not wanting to. However, we had been missed. Loud noises were coming near. We scrambled into our clothes, backwards, and wrong side out. The interlopers poured in upon us. Winking at me, they redressed Bronze, combed his hair and carried him off. The women did the same to me. The party was going full. Bronze was made to tell how the Spirits brought us together. It seemed this would be a defining tale in the tribal history. Even the children sitting in groups were retelling the tale. Bronze was made to repeat it over and over, until he lost his voice. He collapsed on the ground and refused to move or speak.

The men disparaged him. What kind of husband would he be if he couldn't stay on his feet for one night? If he was unable to fulfill his duty they would be more than willing to help their friend, they teased. They proceeded to dance me around the fire, one after the other, placing kisses on my cheek. Bronze roared to his feet, snatching me away into his arms and around the fire. He wiped away all the kisses and replaced them with his own. It was wildly funny. We stopped to have some drink and a bit to eat. We again tried to slip away. This time we grabbed a horse and climbed the hill. Placing a blanket on the ground, we cuddled and kissed. Soon we heard the whoops and hollers, knowing we had been discovered.

The event lasted three days more. The visitors said their goodbyes, leaving lasting blessings on the couple. A visiting holy man, on his departure, foretold of two babes that would come of this union. This he said was a great blessing.

So it was; twin boys were born the next spring only a few weeks after our return to the summer home. The birth went well. Mother and Grandmother were midwives. They taught me herbs and root compounds that would bring strength. The boys were dark eyed like Bronze, but their hair was as fair as corn silk. Bronze was ecstatic. He gazed at his sons nursing loudly at their mother's breasts. He left to find the holy man. He requested a ritual to honor the Great Spirit that had bestowed this blessing on his family and the whole tribe. Twinning was very rare among the Indians, as rare as the birth of a white buffalo calf. Bronze was told to take his family to the top of the hill. There he would dedicate his sons to the Great Spirit at the next full moon. When the word went out of what was to happen, many of the tribe asked Bronze if they too might be allowed to give honor. After all, a tribe is most always family, uncles and cousins. They hoped the good fortune would fall on them as well.

The full moon shone down on the company. It was cool, but not cold. The babes nestled comfortably in their father's arms. The holy man called the circle, and honored the four corners. He passed corn meal to the Ancestors asking that they watch over these babes and fill their minds with the great wisdom known only to the Ancestors. Then the Great Spirit was honored with tobacco. His favor was entreated on behalf of these babes, so that their presence would enrich the family and more honor would be given to the Great Spirit. Last, the "White Buffalo Woman" herself was called upon. She the nurturer, the loving Mother of all, was invoked with sweet grass smudge. A cloud passed the moon just then. Everyone stared. The shadow of a buffalo could be seen. A startled deer broke from cover, bounding down the hillside. The holy man took each babe in turn, blessing and naming them. Their names would be "Running Deer" and "Standing Buffalo." Bronze lifted each boy to the heavens and then walked among the gathering so that all might give and receive blessing. As we slowly descended the hill, the tale was already being woven into the tribal history.

Bedouin Diary

I live in the Negev Desert. My family is Bedouin and we raise camels and goats, moving with the seasons. In the spring, during calving time, we live in caves in the mountains. The rest of the year, we live in our tent. We must move from place to place because there is little water and few grasses for our herds, and we must not let the animals destroy the scant and fragile vegetation.

I have a beautiful, black dog named Hti. He is my close companion, for I have been the only one who has raised him; I alone feed and care for him. It is he that keeps away the snakes and rodents when I sleep. I go each day with my sisters to collect fuel for the fires. Sometimes, when we find a large enough body of water, we strip off our clothes and swim naked. We giggle and splash each other, until duty bids us finish our chores...

... My father has arranged a marriage for me. My husband-to-be is the first son of Sheikh Bani, who is famous throughout the desert for the beautiful horses he breeds. The preparations for the marriage have already begun; they will last from the full moon to the next full moon. Many friends and family will be coming and going. My father has pledged one hundred goats and fiftycamels for my dowry. I will be a great lady.

... Al-Qasr, my husband-to-be, will soon ride in a daring, 3,000-mile race across the desert to the ocean that pits the finest-bred horses from the different desert tribes. Many of the riders and horses never reach the sea. Al-Qasr has won the race in the past, making his father's horses the most prized in all the desert. It is a great honor, and a great expense, to have a mare serviced by one of Sheikh Bani's stallions...

...I shall have servants and spend my time reading and writing poetry to please my husband. I will ride with him on the great horses in his stable and sing ballads of his great works. I will be a gracious hostess to all his visitors and will oversee the cooking of great feasts. Our house will always be full of visitors and family. These are my dreams as the wedding approaches...

...When the day finally comes, the wedding ceremonies turn out to be utterly exhausting. I have hardly had a moment with my husband, which may be a good thing. I feel so shy around him, for he is so strong and beautiful. I hope he will love me; I will have no trouble learning to love him. My grandmother and aunts tease me unmercifully, for tonight will be our first night together as husband and wife. I hope all goes well and that I can soon bear my new husband a son. Dear Allah, please bless me in this prayer. My mother has instructed me in the arts of *Karma Sutra*; I hope I remember everything she said. It's not like I could practice. Allah, please hear my prayer. Let me be a pleasure to my husband and have many children to give honor to his family and mine...

...Well! It was a wonderful night; I think I did all right. Al-Qasr was very content. He kept saying he loved me and that I was beautiful. From the way I feel today, we may well have hit the mark. I can't stop smiling. No one says a word, nor do they tease or make unkind remarks. I am a woman, and a wife, now. Two days hence, Al-Qasr and I will leave my family and travel to our new home. I will be sad to leave my family but it must be done. It is always so with Bedouin women; we must go with our husbands and start a new life. I'm ready. It shall be a great adventure. I might even get to ride one of the great horses of the House of Sheikh Bani. That would be a great honor; I should have to hold my best seat to make my father proud of me...

...My husband has presented me a beautiful white mare as a wedding present. He says I should ride her on our homeward journey, and that only I may water and feed her. I name her Sashi and have introduced my dog Hti to her, for we must all be companions. I feed them together so they will become friends...

...I mounted Sashi today. She is so magnificent that I felt like a queen. Hti walked beside us. I think we made a striking picture: the sleek, white mare, the jet-black dog and me. Everyone stopped to watch as we rode by. When Al-Qasr rode up to join us, he too was smitten. Hti growled at my husband, but I commanded the dog to stop and he did. Hti and Al-Qasr will have to get to know each other better. Hti is very protective of me. When he understands that I love Al-Qasr, he will settle down. It will be nice to have Hti along on the journey to my new home, for he will keep me from being homesick and lonely. I will have to find my own place in this new family. My Sashi and Hti will comfort me. Tomorrow we leave; I'm scared but excited at the same time...

...We have come to our new home Al-Qasr is so gentle, so kind, so attentive to my feelings. I think he understands how hard it is for me to leave my family. He has promised we will make a trip next year to my family. It is sweet of him but not likely, for I will be with child. I have not told him yet, for there are too many new things happening as it is. I pray that the gods grant me a son to carry his father's line...

...Al-Qasr's family is very gracious to me and has helped to prepare our new home. Unlike my own family, which moves every six weeks or less depending on the land and water, Sheikh Bani has made his home and his stables in a year-round oasis. His shepherds move the herds from forage to forage, but the family stays at the oasis with the stable of horses. It is very different from what I am used to; there will be no packing up and moving constantly. It will be lovely to spend more time with my Sashi and Hti. The family won't let me help with the chores yet, though I would like to, for my beloved husband, Al-Qasr, is off practicing for the great race. I must be patient. I ride Sashi every day, exploring the desert all around. Hti is a good trail dog and always gets me home safely even if I lose my way. Sashi, too, always knows the way to the stable and her feed...

> *Out in the desert I go with my friends.*
> *They find the way homeward again*
> *Scrub bush and sand may lead me astray*
> *But my dear friends, they know the way*
> *Starlight and moonshine may lead me away*
> *Hti my black dog, he'll know the way*
> *Sashi, great steed of white*
> *Stately walks on through the dark of the night*
> *Wild board or black snake dare not contend*
> *With my true companions that with me defend*
> *Denizens of the Great Land in dread*
> *Depart the trail that we tread*
> *Hail to Sashi and Hti alike*
> *Together we put up a mighty fight.*

I will put this rhyme to music and sing it for Al-Qasr tonight when he gets home. I may also play my *rababa* and my *shahbbaba,* the flute and strings of my people that I have played since earliest memory. He has not yet heard me play and sing for him. I think I would like him to be in a mellow mood when I tell him I'm with child. He has been so preoccupied with the upcoming race that I have not found the right time to tell him...

...I think my performance went over well. I had hoped to be alone with Al-Qasr, but we had to sup with his father, Sheikh Bani, and his entire family. They insisted that I sing my rhyme and play for them. I think they liked my poem and were very pleased at my voice and talent with the instruments. After I finished, others sang and soon everyone was joining in the ballads. It was really great fun. Al-Qasr's mother and others of the family thanked me and praised my talent, but I still hadn't told my beloved husband the wonderful news. He was so tired he fell asleep after only a little while. I'll try to catch him early in the morning...

...This morning, I think I shocked him with my news. He must have known it was a possibility, but he has his mind on other things right now. Praise the gods that I bear a son to carry the family line. I will seek a wise woman to get herbs and make prayers to Ra and Ishtar and all the gods that can help me. I will ask B'ethel, my sister in-law, who might have the wisdom for this. I don't think Al-Qasr will mind. He might have told me the name of a wise woman himself if he hadn't been so fuddled with the race and all that goes with it. I can make inquires myself...

... My poor husband. Today, I was out riding Sashi, with Hti leading the way. Over a slight rise, we came upon Al-Qasr and his men exercising the horses. When he spotted me, he halted all other activities and rode over on his shining black stallion. He asked if it was safe for me to ride now. I think he wants to lock me away in the house until the babe arrives. Before going back to his practice, he made me promise that I would do no racing or rough riding. B'ethel gave me the name of a wise woman today. She and I will go there after the meal tonight...

...B'ethel and I go to the baked clay hut of the wise woman, who lived in a distant part from the oasis. The herbs and flowers of the garden could be smelled long before we reached the vine-covered door. The wise woman has given me herbs, tea and a fine clay powder with minerals to help prepare me for the birth. I am so excited and pray every day for the health of our child. I have asked the other women of the family to join in the prayer as well; they are happy to be included. Al-Qasr told me he too has consulted his father's wise man. I guess we have left no stone unturned; it is good to have the gods on our side in this...

...The great race is set for the next lunar cross, that night in the vast desert sky when the moon beams expand from four sides in a cross of full moon light. I will watch the start of the race, and then pray that Al-Qasr will be safe. The wait will be difficult, for it will take about 85 days to make the 3,000-mile journey across the desert. The Sheikh will send riders to keep us posted as to the progress of the race. I must be a good wife and think of nothing but victory for Al-Qasr, for any other thought could invite calamity on the riders. The gods alone will choose the winner. I will seek their favor with many offerings and prayers; that is how I will support this important event. ..

...I made a pilgrimage to the sacred shrine with prayers and offerings early this morning. The other women of the family joined me. We stopped to visit the wise woman when returning home, but I was not comforted with her words. I must keep this to myself and force my thoughts to be hopeful...

...I saw my beloved husband off with a kiss and a prayer today. The throng of people at the starting point was more than I could have imagined in my wildest dreams. Thankfully the Sheikh arranged for a platform, for otherwise, I'm sure we would have been trampled in the crowd. Colorful banners flapped in the wind, symbols of the tribes who were racing. The sight was thrilling and frightening all at the same time. The magnificent horses were snorting and pawing the earth. When the flag dropped, the whole line of animals and brightly dressed riders seemed to fly into the air. The thunder of their departure rang in my ears. I have never before been part of anything as grand as today's festival...

... I'm on edge. My heart pounds with apprehension as riders bring news of the progress of the race. Every day, another message arrives. Two of the riders have died already from accidents across the rough terrain. The weather is holding well for the riders; the temperature has not reached its maximum, for it is still spring in the desert. The riders are in the mountains somewhere, but I am unfamiliar with the route so do not know how far away they are. I only know that they must cover many miles across mostly desert, all the way to the ocean. Another rider has been attacked by a wild boar; he is not expected to live. Thirty-five riders started the race; now only 27 remain, three have died...

... I received a note from Al-Qasr today, telling me not to worry. Nothing will keep him from me, and our child. The note contained a lovely pressed flower. I have never beheld one like it; he wrote that he had said he found it in the oasis where he stopped for food and water. He writes that his love for me keeps him focused when the trail is hard and monotonous. I cannot reply, for there is no way to reach him. The riders who bring the news were sent out months ago to wait along the route and pass the information back to us...

....Every evening, the family gathers to present prayers and offerings, and to discuss any news that has come in. It will take months for the race to finish. My sister-in-law assures me that the race will finish before our child is born, but I have my doubts, for they must reach the ocean and then return. I felt the babe quicken today. Another rider has been eliminated; his horse fell and broke its leg; it had to be put down. I have put the race out of my mind, for if I think about it constantly, I would only worry the more. The Sheikh, my father-in-law, came to me this evening and spoke with me for a long time. He is very kind, and is anxious about his grandchild and heir. He confessed to me that he probably should not have allowed his son to partici-pate in the race this year, even though it was vital to the stable. Another could have been sent in Al-Qasr's stead. This would be his son's last race. Al-Qasr was now head of his own family, and as such, was responsible for our well-being. He also told me that no matter what happened, my son and I would always be taken care of. I'm sure he meant to comfort me, but the truth is I'm scared. The wise woman's words and now those of the Sheikh have disturbed me no end. I have tried to put them out of my head, for only the gods hold our destiny. No mortal can change that...

... My body is growing heavy with the life inside. I work daily with the *sutra,* yoga-like stretches, to keep supple and strong. My rides on Sashi are more stately and less wild than before; she seems to understand. It was decided that she would be bred to a great stallion as soon as possible, for I will soon be busy with the babe. The timing could not be better. The Sheikh has consulted his studbook to choose the right bloodlines. Sashi will produce a great foal, just as I will produce a great son...

... The time seems to drag. It is at night that I miss Al-Qasr the most. My days are full of work and other people, but after the evening meal, when all go to their separate dwellings, I really feel the loneliness. Hti comes and puts his head in my lap, trying to comfort me...

... The wise woman told me that the babe would come on the next moon cycle. I am so happy, but Al-Qasr is still somewhere far away, risking his life every day. He is faced with the tremendous heat and chilling nights of the desert. Messages come less frequently now, for the riders have completed half of their journey. The Sheikh plans to go to the finish line at the ocean port by boat. He will leave tomorrow and travel by horseback for some time before he reaches the ocean; there he will board a ship and travel along the vast coast to the finish line. If the birth of the child were not imminent, I would have been allowed to accompany him. Once the race is over, he will bring Al-Qasr and the horses back by boat, as has been done for centuries before...

... I think a secret is being kept from me. Perhaps it is just my imagination, but talk changes when I come into a room. Maybe they just don't want to worry me because of the babe. The Horseman is in the night sky now. I feel the babe lower and lower...

... I have been too busy to write in my diary. My son Sette is dark and round and just too beautiful for words. When I first held him in my arms, I felt a joy so great I thought I might burst, so tremendous was the feeling of love. No one deserves to be so happy and blessed. His tiny body is so perfect; his little hand curls around my finger. When I hold him to my breast, it is a true miracle. He is sleeping now, so I have time to write and listen to him breathe in his cradle...

... Al-Qasr is here now, but he cannot see his son. His eyes are closed forever; he is on his death pallet. The family is stunned, and if I didn't have Sette, I would not be able to cope. My beloved husband had suffered a terrible fall when his horse was startled by a desert snake and shied suddenly. They were traveling so fast that neither had time to react until it was too late. His head hit a rock and many bones were broken. He was given hyssop for the pain and brought to the coast in a cart. The Sheikh, who had arrived at the port shortly after the accident, didn't leave Al-Qasr's side, cursing himself for letting his son embark on such a dangerous ride. I tell my dear father-in-law that the gods pick and choose; it is not for us to understand. I can tell he is not comforted by my words...

... I sit by the bed upon which Al-Qasr's broken body lies. Sette is in my arms as I tell my beloved husband all about our son. I hope he can hear me. I sometimes see a white wisp of ether around the body and I think his soul is trying to find the way out...

... I went to the wise woman today and asked her to come and help Al-Qasr make his journey. I could not ask his father; he is just too distraught to think clearly and I cannot let my husband go on suffering this way. I have enlisted the help of B'ethel and the other women; they agree about what must be done. Tonight we will send the Sheikh on an errand to get him out of the house so that we can help my husband's soul...

...It is done. We women gathered around my husband's body, five of us on either side. The wise woman directed from the head; I was at his feet. Sette slept peacefully in the corner. We covered the body with a silk cloth woven with gold. The wise woman said the prayers as we gently raised the body from its resting place. She swept the soul out from under him, and we then put the soul on the cloth of gold, carried it out the door and watched as the white ether floated away into the night sky. We then prepared the body for burning by washing it and rubbing with scented herbs. I had to stop to nurse Sette when he woke while the others worked on. The cloth of gold was wrapped around the body, and then linen cords were used to secure it.

Outside, the pyre was being prepared by the male members of the family. I rejoined the group after Sette finished his meal. Then I took some paint and drew a horse on the shroud. Others added their mementos. His mother tucked a small toy from his childhood. After everyone had spoken or prayed near the body, I placed a lovely flower in the cord that bound his body. The Sheikh had returned as we were finishing the preparations. He sat in the corner with Sette in his arms, tears streaming down his face. The mighty ruler crooned a lament to the child. I tried not to look at him as I was not sure if my father-in-law understood we had assisted Al-Qasr's soul in leaving his broken body, but I would not have done differently...

... The pyre was lit tonight at midnight. The moon was still in full light and the Horseman made his way across the sky. Al-Qasr is riding with him now. A birth, a death, and still the rider holds his course. The family is still in mourning. I am told it will go on for at least a month or more. People come and go. I have Sette to tend to so I come and go as I can. Everyone is so kind to us. They all bring gifts for me, and the child. I worry about Sheikh Bani, who seems to have aged suddenly. He takes his son's death very hard, and wishes to see Sette at all hours of the day and night. I take my son to him, for it is little enough to do to console him in his grief. He will have to be Sette's father now...

...Sometimes the loneliness is so deep in me I wonder what to do. I want to be happy for my son so that I can show him joy and love. I must tuck away my grief inside my heart and be happy that I have my son to keep me busy...

...Life is getting back to normal, The Sheikh has called a family meeting for tomorrow night. I have a feeling he wants to settle Al-Qasr's affairs. That may mean he has a plan for Sette and me. I pray that I can agree to whatever he comes up with, for though I really don't want to hurt my father-in-law's feelings, I will not be manipulated either. Who would have thought life would come to this after such a lovely wedding. I place my life in the hands of the gods, for who are we mortals to say what should be...

... I have a new husband. Just like that, I float on the whim of fate. Hannal is Al-Qasr's brother. He has not yet arrived and I have never met him, or even heard of him before today. The story I was told last night is this: Hannal has been on pilgrimage with a holy man for some years. He studies the herbs and the healing way. I can only guess that the family never really understood his ways. We shall see. He has been called home to take his place as his brother's replacement, to serve as my husband and Sette's father. Please, gods, give me strength to make the best of this. I must agree for Sette's sake. I will make a trip to the wise woman to seek her advice on how to prepare for this new event later today...

... I feel so much better. The wise woman knows Hannal. She thinks I am very lucky indeed to have two such extraordinary men in my life. Hannal is very spiritual; he is a seer, a holy man. He will be gentle and loving and teach Sette many things: the stars, the crops, the herbs of healing. The Sheikh will teach my son about horses, but Hannal will teach him joy and love in all things. She said I should approach this union with an open heart, for he is a very different man from Al-Qasr. She asked me if I would bring Hannal to see her when he comes home. I told her I would try, though I had no idea how he might take the invitation. When I made to leave, she gave me some spices to burn in preparation for my new life...

...Now I have such an adventure to look forward to. I mean to put my whole heart into this new relationship. Sette will do well, for I know that for he is so greatly loved already. He is growing very strong, attacking my nipple with such fervor I shudder. When he has drunken his fill, he relaxes in such contented sleep that my heart just feels such tenderness for him. I'm sure this may be true for all mothers but these are my words and I want to remember always the wonder of this child. I know that someday he will be grown and far away from me; these words will evoke the truest picture of this moment in time. As he lies there in his cradle, a sweet smile on his lips, his lashes brushing his round cheek, a tiny tear glitters just at the corner of his eye. His mouth makes a gentle sucking noise. My first-born son, I wonder what he will become when he is a man...

...Hannal has come home. He is so ethereal, he frightens me a bit. He is not unkind in any way; I just don't know him. We had a simple wedding, at least I think we have. The words spoken were unknown to me but I got their gist. Hannal and I have not been intimate. We are just getting used to each other. Hti and Sashi adore him, for he has a gentle way with all creatures. Even Sette gazes into his eyes in rapture when Hannal holds him. I, too, am falling under his spell. He is so serene that when he looks at me, I feel a warm vibration around my whole being, as if he is wrapping his energy around me.

Hannal gives me his undivided attention, and asks me to walk with him. When we walk together, he lifts Sette onto his back and we hike into the hills, Hti at our heels. Hannal is patient as he points out plants and birds and rocks. He tells me that everything has a soul. He picks up a rock and has me put it in my hand and feel the heat of it. It is that way with everything, everything. Sometimes a hawk will speak to Hannal from a tree and my new husband will answer back...

...I am falling under a spell. Am I a fickle person for loving this brother of my husband or am I divinely blessed to have the good fortune to love two totally different men? I honor the memory of Al-Qasr, but he is gone from me. In reality, he was always gone from me. That race took his time and his life from me. Hannal and I have spent more time together in the few weeks since we met than Al-Qasr and I had in all of our marriage. How strange that is. I am ready now to share my deepest feelings with Hannal...

...Hannal watches as I suckle Sette. My new husband touches my garment, pulling it away to show my glowing skin beneath. In his hands he holds a lump of clay and begins shaping it with his long, graceful fingers. Ever so tenderly, he copies the curves of my neck and shoulders; then Sette, too, becomes part of the figure. Hannal's hands are so knowing, his creation is wonderful. He has the artist's eye. The moment is so intimate, the love is so enveloping, I feel it to my very soul. He wants me to be ready when he comes to me. I think I'm ready. He is waiting for a sign that his brother gives his blessing...

....Hannal and I were putting Sette into his cradle when a blast of wind blew the curtains into the room. A night bird caught off guard tumbled in on the wind and flew dizzily around the room. The bird managed to right itself and swooped out of the window, almost as suddenly as it had arrived. My husband and I faced one another and smiled. I turned to the still-wet statue of mother and child and as I gently ran my finger along its smooth surface, Hannal touched my shoulder. He drew me into his arms and became my husband...

... He was right. The time of our joining was perfect, for I now carry Sette's playmate in my womb. Hannal had studied the Tantra and is very amazing from all perspectives. I had thought I was very happy with Al-Qasr but now I hardly remember our brief life together. Hannal fills all my thoughts. Our connection is so strong that we speak to one another without words. His thoughts are in my head; I know he can hear me even when we are apart...

... I have visited the wise woman. She laughs at me. "Didn't I tell you so?" I responded that I had no idea what she had been talking about then, but that now I knew. "Hannal is a great man," she tells me. I tell her that I have asked him to visit her, which he has agreed to do. At the moment, I tell her, the Sheikh has involved him in many details of the family affairs. As I prepare to leave, she gives me exotic spices and herbs. When I ask what they are for, she tells me that I will know when the time comes. She will tend me at my birthing as before. I give her a hug...

... Sashi has thrown a magnificent foal. I was able to be there for the event. The new little stallion emerged, still in the sac. The grooms tore away the filmy cover. His eye lashes fluttered and he struggled to his feet. Gray and dappled now, his mature color is yet unknown. Amazing! The wobbly new foal looked at all of us, standing there as if to say "Hello! Who are you?" He then turned to his mother and nuzzled along her flank until he found the teat. Sashi turned her head and explored his body with her tongue, taking in the scent of him as she dried him off. It was so beautiful I almost cried. I felt a delicious bunching in my own belly as the miracle resonated within...

... Hannal and I have told the family of the pending birth; they are all very pleased. Sheikh Bani gave me a firm hug, his face beaming. I think he feels that he has had a dispensation from the sorrow and guilt he felt at taking Al-Qasr from his family. I think the Sheikh finally can experience the sense that the gods are smiling on him. Sette is walking now and the Sheikh is personally undertaking his grandson's education. This is nice, for it gives Hannal and me time together. My wonderful husband helps me with body work to strengthen my stamina for the upcoming birth. It has been suggested that I will have more than one. So I will need all my strength. Hannal is a holy man; he has taught me to meditate. I find it very invigorating. We try to find moments to work together at least three times a day. Sometimes we spend those minutes inside, at others we take walks in the hills around the oasis. It is so relaxing to look out on the flocks of sheep and goats that I feel a oneness with the universe...

...There is so much to learn and understand. Every time I make a new discovery, it seems there are dozens of other things I want to know and learn about. Hannal laughs at my eagerness, for he had not known that a woman could be so interested in spiritual things. It was not that he thought women were not intelligent; it was more that they were so involved in life at the basic need level that they had no time to do more than that. After all, women are already responsible for so much. I tell him I can do many things at the same time. When I croon Sette to sleep, I can also think of spiritual things. When I arrange meals and do housework, I can meditate, and when I stitch a new cloak, I can dream of the oneness of all things. He thinks it amazing and loves me the more...

... I found my diary today. It has been a long time, and as I read what I wrote all those years ago, I have to marvel at all that has gone on since life was so simple. Sette is a young man now and all the other children look to him as their leader. Sheikh Bani is an old man and Sette is the heir apparent. Hannal has abdicated in favor of Sette, for he has no interest in running the family affairs. He is a holy man and prefers healing work and spiritual understanding to material issues. Sette has a real feel for business and thrives under the training provided by his grandfather. My son travels all over the country and even across the ocean to buy and sell. We all sit around as he tells of the adventures he has had. Sometimes I think he must make up some of the stories about places he goes. It is hard to believe people really live as he tells it...

... Sheikh Bani is not able to travel with Sette any longer, so Sette has a trusted assistant, Sarif, the son of B'ethel. Sarif is three years older than Sette. They both seem so young to me, but that is the way of the world. It is the young men that must go away form home and make their way in the world. I must say Sette is a very strong and serious young man. Yet he still likes to play tricks on me just as he did as a child. That makes me happy, for it is not good to take life too seriously and we never know when it will be over. Sette has been told of his father's death at the young age of 19. Sette always says he has too much to learn to die now. He is 17, so young yet so wise for his age. I am a proud mother...

... Our twin girls are to be married soon. Hannal and I have been approached by several families for matches. The Sheikh is involved in the negotiations; it does him good for it has been difficult for him to give up most of the family affairs to Sette. He knows it is the right thing to do, and now acts as a trusted adviser, providing valuable advice based on years of experience to Sette and all the family...

...It worked out to be a double wedding. I don't know how they will manage being separated now, for twins are a world unto themselves. The families they are to marry into live far apart, which concerns me. I think it will put a strain on my girls, but I must put my fears aside and pray for their happiness. Now I know what my own family went through at my wedding all those years ago. I hope I have forgotten no one in the invitations. The Sheikh has spared no expense for his granddaughters. I am so grateful for the help, for I think the whole world is coming to my doorstep for this event. The celebration will go on for a month or more. My dear husband Hannal is helpful but a bit lost in all the fuss. He has never kept up the family connection as the Sheikh does, for his connections are more ethereal than physical...

...There are many roads a man may travel. The graceful merging of one with another is the true character of the man, or woman for that matter. I, too, have traveled many paths. I have carried nine babies in my womb. Some were only with us for a short time; each was a blessing in our lives. Hannal is a wise and much-loved husband. His strength and spirituality have brought such comfort to my heart when we had to release the souls that were not meant to stay with us and grow to old age in this life-time...

...Some years ago, the Sheikh was implored by a cousin to become involved in a war over water rights. It seems wars are always over water in this time and within our territory. The strife took many lives and when the dust settled, Sheikh Bani had become an old man. Hannal and I were there to welcome him when he returned home at last. We entered his house; he sat in the dark until we lit the lamps and brightened the gloom. We kissed him and made pleasantries, but we could tell the gloom was not merely physical.

Our beloved father's heart was heavy. Finally he spoke; I think it was to Hannal that he addressed his words. "Family honor has forced me to do a great injustice." He explained that the issue of water rights was clearly with the other side. Yet his family ties had made it necessary to side with his cousin against the rightful owner. Bani's participation put the power of a great force with the cousin; they had won even though they were in the wrong. The Sheikh turned to Hannal and asked how a man could live a good life when these choices were put upon him. Do the right thing and lose the family, the allies needed for future protection, or side with the family in a false endeavor and commit a travesty against other people in the name of family.

Hannal walked around for a few minutes. He then put his hand on his father's shoulder and spoke quietly. "Man is put on this earth to make such choices all the time. The judgment as to right or wrong is out of our hands. We can only do the best we can with what we are given. We are given a set of rules to help us make the choices but rules do not fit every need. You are neither the first nor will you be the last to face such a decision. Be comforted that you are not perfect; only the gods are on that level. We are mortal and must live with our confusion. It is enough that we try to do the right thing, the best as we see it. Be at peace, Father. Let your soul rest; do not carry this burden. It serves no purpose to dwell on it, for what is done is done. Learn from it and let it go. New challenges are sure to come along soon enough."

Hannal's words seemed to comfort Sheikh Bani, who nevertheless continued to wear his years and experiences like a cloak of despair. Hannal brooded over the situation for some time afterward. He confided to me his concern as to whether or not he had given the best advice to his father. I countered that he might do well to take his own advice. Hannal had done the best he could at the time. It seems to me this question in its many disguises affects us in more life situations than we would wish to count...

...Some time after his grandfather returned from the water rights dispute, Sette was to set out on a great adventure. He was to travel to all the strongholds of the family and present himself as the heir apparent taking on the alliances of the retired Sheikh. All of his energy and attention were directed to this event. The war faded into the background. The Sheikh was full of advice for his grandson and trusted companion, Sarif, before their departure. I breathed a little sigh of relief, for both father and grandfather had other occupations to divert them as Hannal had to cover the work of Sette, while the younger was away. I prayed that all war would stay far from our door, for I had other young sons to think of. Young men always seem to see glory in battle, while mothers see only the broken bodies or death. I guess that is why death is women's work; it is up to us to prepare the bodies and send the souls to the next level. It allows men to pretend that death does not occur. Perhaps I'm being too hard on them with such words. It is the husbands and fathers who are charged with the responsibility of providing safe homes and food for their families. They do the best they can. We all do the best we can...

... Sette carries the robe of Sheikh now. I think he makes a good leader. His prowess as a merchant is already legendary. My first-born son prefers peace to war and that is good. He has had to deal with some uprisings, and for that, he has relied on his younger brother, Abdul, for battle strategies. L'Hannal, our youngest son, is the keeper of the studbooks and manages the stables. I think Sheikh Bani would be proud of his family. Al-Qasr and Hannal have left a strong dynasty behind. I continue to shepherd the flock in my way..

... I pick up my diary again. How life has wended its unique pattern. Years ago, Hannal slipped from this world as gently as he lived, his long hair, uncut as was tradition for holy men, testament to his many years of grace. I have mourned two husbands and so many family members. They have stepped into a new adventure while I must finish my work here. How strange it seems that it is I, the "new" wise woman, to whom the young girls come for herbs and medicine. I am the one to attend the births and deaths now. The men come to me for insights on war and peace. I hope I can give comfort to all who come searching. As I read my words from the beginning, I think of how amazing life really is. I cherish the thoughts and actions of my life here written. I have been truly blessed...

Book 3

Rituals and Lists

Introduction to
Book 3: Rituals and Lists

This book starts with the list that Dan Churchill mentioned in his foreword. I refer to this list in my work in soul retrieval. The some of the levels may have other names, for example: The 25th level has many names in different religious venues. One additional name, the Crystal Cave, I will mention here. The white light of near-death-experience originates in the Crystal Cave. I wrote about it in the dream chapter. It is that light that guides the souls during transition from the physical to the spiritual realms. Do not feel that if you have other names for some of the levels mine are right and yours are wrong. It doesn't work that way. There is no rigidity here; the list I present here works for me and with all things. You may want to fit it to your vision.

Some of the rituals presented in the following section were developed to help individual clients with past life issues that were intruding on the present life: The sleep ritual was designed for a young man with a sleep issue that came with him from a life in which he was a soldier. As that soldier, he had fallen asleep on sentry duty and the enemy had overrun his camp, resulting in the death of his compatriots. That trauma carried forward as insomnia.

The resulting ritual allowed him to confront that soul knowledge and move past it. Not all sleep issues are related in this way, but the format of this ritual can be personalized to fit other scenarios. A person may feel other angels or guides are more compatible with the need and that is fine. Again, none of this is written in stone. The rituals are more like family recipes that maybe spiced according to one's own taste.

The separation ritual was for a client who had a very strong emotional attachment to a particular place. What really upset her was the diametrically opposed depth of those emotions from peace and tranquility to pain and horror to the point of tears, that being at this place evoked in her. The answer and ritual came when we uncovered a past life as a Native American. She had lived on this land with her family in joy and happiness until one day the tribe was attacked and destroyed. That event lay in her soul memory and each time she returned to the place where the conflict had occurred, she was bombarded with the emotional attachment.

She took the ritual and some small statues of her power animals and did the ritual on the ground where her emotions were trapped; she was able to separate from that memory in unconditional love. It was an experience her soul had to have to move on to its path. Now, after the ritual, she can reconnect to the pleasure of the place without the intense emotional upset.

I will state again there is no right or wrong way to do rituals. It is the intent with which they are done that is the important element. The ultimate goal is "for the Highest and Best Good."

The 33 Soul Levels
Upper and Lower / Gia

33 Levels Up

33 Godhead

32 Seraphim

31 Cherubim

30 Counsel ("Grandfather")

29 Dominions
Archangel Zadkiel

28 Archangel Michael
Loving Realm

27 Archangel Raphael
Healing Realm & Balance

26 Virtues (my sister)
Archangel Haniel

25 Soul Recovery (Purgatory)
Planetary Logos

24 Shaman, Healers

23 Faeries

22 Gnomes
Earth / Cardinal Point North

21 Sylphs

20 Jesus, Sananda
(Ascended Masters)

19 Archangel Barchiel

18 Sandalphon, Safiroth

33 Levels Down

– 33 Garden

– 32 Extraterrestrials / Grays

– 31 Angel Israel

– 30 Angel of Death

– 29 Kakabel

– 28 Angel Suriel

– 27 Incubi, Succubi

– 26 Semyaza

– 25 Archangel Raziel

– 24 Archangel Ariel
Archangel Raquel

– 23 Lilith, Samuel

– 22 Annanuki

– 21 New Souls, Angels

– 20 Reptilians

– 19 Archangel Verchiel

– 18 Angel Kafziel

33 Levels Up

17	Temple (Ascended masters)
16	Archangel Metatron
15	Muhammad
14	Undines
13	Archangel Uriel
12	Angel Ramiel
11	Over-soul
10	Black Hole
09	Time Lords
08	Rehabilitation (Hell)
07	Archangel Gabriel
06	Primary Guides / Angels
05	Spirit / Faerie
04	Principalities
03	Akashic Records
02	Buddha
01	Crystalline Merkabah

33 Levels Down

– 17	Salamanders Fire, Cardinal Point South
– 16	Archon
– 15	Valkyries
– 14	Archangel Zadchiel (Animals)
– 13	Elohim
– 12	Angel Anael
– 11	Archangel Moroni
– 10	Angel Nuriel
– 09	Hall of Contracts
– 08	Lords of Karma
– 07	Archangel Lucifer
– 06	Angel Lahash
– 05	Teaching (Old Souls)
– 04	Creative Force
– 03	Star Beings
– 02	Elementals
– 01	Nephilium

Gia (Earth)

The Law of One

We are all one.
When one is harmed, all are harmed
When one is helped, all are helped
Therefore, in the name of my being
which is one with all there is
and is all powerful and all loving
and is with all the Masters
and with the Christ.

*I ask for that which is for the highest good
of all concerned to happen here*

*On the physical plane, the greatest beauty
On the emotional plane, the most profound joy
In the world of the mind, the greatest illumination
And in the spirit, unity*

I offer thanks that this is done
So Be It!

Body Healing

I call down the healing hands of the cosmic Christ:
Balance my spin, my rotation and colors;
Prepare me for the tasks that I must do today.
Cleanse my crystals, my chakras,
My seven layers of consciousness
My physical plant: eyes, ears, nose, throat, heart, lungs, liver,
spleen, bladder, gall bladder, stomach, intestines;
Kidneys, pancreas, reproductive organs, thymus;
Hypothalamus, pituitary, pineal, thyroid, and adrenal glands;
Cerebrum, cerebellum, frontal, occipital and temporal lobes;
Corpus luteum, hippocampus, medulla oblongata, brain stem.

Every day I am healthier and stronger.
Every five years, each cell in my body is renewed. Let each new
cell that comes on line be as pure as on the day I was born.
Balance my *chi*, my *uvarta*, my *prana*.

Cleanse all the systems of my body: autonomic and somatic;
Skeletal, muscular, central nervous, endocrine, circulatory;
Respiratory, vascular, hepatic, herpatic, lymphatic, immune;
Digestive, elimination, ocular, auditory, olfactory, reproductive.

Thank you, dear Angels, for all you do for me!

We expect our bodies to operate on auto-pilot. They will do much better when we focus our attention on them. If you have areas of concern, add extra focus to those areas. For instance, stomach discomfort can be specified and so on. Each time you name an individual part, you are sending energy to that part. More blood flows to it and it responds.

Take care of your body, and it will take care of you during your stay on this Planet Earth.

Gardening with Elementals

The "job" of the elementals is to create beautiful gardens on earth, and to hold form and place in this dimension. The elementals are the uncombined spirit, the base unit of life here. They are here to work with us. Please ask and honor them. Each spot of earth has an elemental in residence, unless toxic burn has caused it to flee. Working with elementals can be a great benefit to both you and the elementals. The elementals include, but are not limited to the Sylphs of the East or air, the Undines of the West or water, the Salamanders of the South or fire, the Gnomes of the North or Earth.

Elementals vibrate at a different level than we do. Many people are unable to see them, just as they are not able to see the angels. This, of course, doesn't mean that the elementals aren't there. If, for some reason, they have abandoned the soil you are working on, call them back. They will come. It is their joy to be summoned, to work in harmony with you to create a lovely garden. (If you wish to learn more about the elementals, The Findhorn Community has a web site that discusses them.)

The more you work with your elemental, the more likely you will catch a glimpse of it. Enticing it to help your garden grow abundantly only requires a request. If you are a dowser, you may use your tools (pendulum, rods) to interact with the elemental of your garden.

Questions to ask your elemental or elementals:

What plants would be best to plant here?

Does the soil need nutrients?

Are there pests that I need to work with?

Can you bring birds here that would be appropriate?

These are just some of the issues you can ask assistance for from the elementals. There will be more that are significant to your garden. Think outside the box. (The chemical box to be sure.) If you are having infestation issues, please work first with your elementals. They may solve the problem in most creative ways.

I encourage everyone to honor the elementals. They are most happy if you acknowledge them. Their talent is vast. You and your garden, be it flowers or vegetables, will respond positively to this collaboration. It is not too much to ask that your produce go from yellow ribbon to blue ribbon, if you are willing to work in harmony with your elementals!

To all the Elementals that reside here
I give honor and praise
I ask your help in creating.
This garden is our venture,
Please bestow your talents here.
Guide me to the choices
That benefit all.

Family Prayer

I call down the white, gold light of unconditional Love.
I call it into my head, into my heart and around my body.
I send that light of unconditional Love to _____(mate).
Let him/her feel the warm vibration of the unconditional Love
In his/her head, in the heart and around the body.
Then sent that light of unconditional Love to our children.
Let them feel the warm vibration of unconditional Love,
In their heads, in their hearts and around their bodies.
(Perhaps add a line here for other special people)
Let them feel that warm vibration and
know they are part of a family.

Then bring the unconditional Love back to me.
The perfect Love, the I AM Love.
The whole family is surrounded in the perfect Love,
The Unconditional Love,
The I AM Love
Send down a violet circle of protection around the whole family.
Call the quarters: Air in the East, Water in the West, Fire in the
South, Earth in the North.
We honor Mother Earth, from whose womb we are delivered and
to whose bosom we return.
She who provides the most beautiful garden in which we live.
We honor the God/Goddess in each of us
And all the Gods that are one God.

Removing Addictions

The following ritual was originally presented by Rev. Sharon Forrest and modified by David Stanger, who wrote one of the forewords for this book, and who gave me permission to adapt it for this book.

You can use a crystal to remove alcohol, tobacco and related items addiction. First ascertain that the client really **wants to quit the habit.** I generally ask them to come to me. However, first ask your client to say a silent prayer for this work to be done while you say your own prayer.

1. Use one large quartz crystal, or another type of crystal. Intent that the crystal be used to remove addiction is most important.

2. Program the crystal with intent to remove the addiction for the specific item and set aside the dependency, addiction or habit.

3. If the client is sure he or she wishes to quit, ask him/her to write the name of the addictive substance or habit on a piece of paper. Then use body testing (kinesiology) to check for good and bad responses. Ask the client to hold the paper in the palm of his/her hand, then hold the hand against the thymus gland with the left hand. Use the client's right arm to test for acceptance of the substance. There should be a negative response with the arm (weakened response).

4. Have the client tear the paper and then burn it (symbolic). If it is tobacco, the client can use an actual cigarette.

5. Have the client sit in a chair. Use the crystal, after programming it to withdraw the dependency on the substance. Bring the crystal close the thymus and turn it in a counter-clockwise direction. In doing so, you are "unscrewing" the dependency. Keep this up until the dependency has been cleared, about four to five minutes; you will feel the change. Ask the client to tell you about any emotions or feelings during the process.

6. Reprogram the crystal to put in the love of God and a thought form that will make the client feel very sick should he or she use the substance again. For this, turn the crystal in a clockwise direction until the process feels complete.

7. Check with the client to see how he or she feels.

Sleep Ritual

I have used the following ritual to balance my energies before bedtime and get a more restful sleep. This ritual was created for a client who was struggling with past life issues, as described in the introduction to this section.

1. Create a sacred space with candles, crystals, and any items that have meaning for you.

2. Call the circle, which means scribing a circle around you and your sacred place with one arm, stating: "This is my sacred place. All energies and entities that are not beneficial will leave now."

3. Reach your dominant hand up to the Universe and say: "You are the Universe." Cross it over your chest, saying: "The power," then stretch it back across to the other side (like the sign of the cross in most religions), "The glory"

4. Call the quarters: "Air in the East, Water in the West, Fire in the South, Earth in the North."

5. Then say: "I invite the Sylphs of the East, the Undines of the West, the Salamanders of the South, and the Gnomes of the North, to come and hold place and form on this plan."

6. Follow this by repeating three times: "I call Archangel Ra-ziel."

7. Then repeat three to five times: "I ask that all impediments to sleep be removed."

8. After that, state: "I represent Gia, the planet Earth, and Mars, the planet of war. I ask that all impediments to sleep be removed." (Repeat three times)

9. Then repeat three times: "I call Archangel Metatron to take me to the Hall of Remembering, down the steps to the door. I put the memory and the pain on the door that is sealed with three plugs. With the help of Archangel Metatron, I remove each plug. The pain and memory that prevent my sleep stay on the door."

10. Then say: "I open the door to a clear path, free of pain, full of restful sleep."

11. Finish by stating: My ritual is done.
All entities and energies
may go about their business
until I call again
Go in peace and do my bidding,
for so it must be.

12. Then open the circle and put out the candle.

May your sleep be undisturbed.

Separation Ritual

This ritual will help you separate from a situation or person which no longer serves your highest good.

1. Write down on a piece of paper all the words you need to say to the person or situation from which you wish to separate.

2. Create a sacred place, with items that are important to you: crystals, flowers, incense, tools, a picture, bowls, bells, drums, stones, and anything that feels right.

3. Light one or more candles.

4. Call a circle, which means scribing a circle around you and your sacred place with one arm, stating: "This is my sacred place, all energies and entities that are not beneficial may leave now!"

5. Then make the sign of the cross, stating: "You are the Universe, the Power and the Glory."

6. Then call the Quarters: "Air in the East, Water in the West, Fire in the South, Earth in the North."

7. The next step is calling in all your angels and guides. You
    may have a special connection to one or another of the angels
    or archangels. Call them in, too.
    "I call Archangel Michael of the loving realm."
    "I call Archangel Raphael of the healing realm."
    "I call all my personal guides and angels."
    "I call all the Ascended Masters, and all others who would
    benefit me."

8. Then:
    "I represent Venus, the planet of love."
    "I represent Mercury, the planet of speed."
    "I ask that healing in love come to me with speed." (repeat
    three times)
    "I ask that this separation in love benefit all." (repeat three
    times)
    "Let the words I have written in love and separation reach
    the Universe" (repeat three times)

9. Rip the paper on which you wrote the person or object from
    which you wished to separate into small strips and burn them
    in a bowl. As the words burn, picture the person, thing or
    situation from which you are separating. As the flames go out,
    so goes the picture. You can later bury or spread the ashes.

10. Finally, open the circle, stating: "My ritual is done. All ener-
    gies and entities may leave now. Until I call again in the Ul-
    tama name, go in peace and do my bidding. For so it must be.
    Ho!"

Follow-up to
Soul Retrieval Ritual

Over the years, soul retrieval has provided me with interesting and beneficial experiences. One particular client had two soul parts that we searched for: one was found on the +30th level with a lovely and graceful star-being of Pleiadian ilk.

When conducting soul retrievals, I use my dowsing tool to determine what soul part to look for, and then dowse my list of 33 upper and lower levels map to locate any splintered parts. I then go in (astral travel) to get the parts and integrate them with the rest of the person's soul. Once brought together again, it is important to make sure that the retrieved parts remain together. I have created, with the help of one of my clients, the following ritual to encourage the soul parts to remain together and intact. You can adapt the ritual to personalize it for your particular situation.

1. After a soul retrieval, first write down the following on a piece of paper: Soul part(s) retrieved

    Gender
    Age
    Level or location

You may choose to combine all the soul parts at one time or honor them individually. Tune into this information.

2. Prepare a sacred space in which to conduct the ritual. Bring into that space candles, crystals, and items of special importance to you, as well as drums, rattles or bells.

3. Light a candle. Focus on the flame as a representative of Spirit. Then take three deep breaths, pressing the center of your chest to push out additional air. Hold your breath, then inhale deeply.

4. Draw a circle in the air, about five feet in diameter depending on the length of your arm, around yourself and your items, stating: "All energies and entities that are not beneficial may leave now."

5. Call the quarters: Air in the East, Water in the West, Fire in the South, Earth in the North.

6. Honor each or all of the soul parts that have returned to you. Acknowledge your love for them. Thank them for returning to you. Promise to do your best to keep them safe. Chant, drum, rattle or make other sounds, with the intent of honoring them, for one minute.

7. Open the circle, and thank all the guides and spirits.

Continue the ritual every day for fourteen days, and then repeat monthly, as you deem appropriate.

(This ritual was created with the help of Flowing Water, after her experience of soul retrieval with Ginger.)

Visualization

We are creators. We can dream. Those dreams can become reality, just as I created the "garden" in my mind and shared with you in Book 1. Many others have had such experiences as well. The technique of visualization is used by talented professionals in many fields. Athletes at the top of their games visualize winning plays. Motivational speakers use the same type of internal encouragement by visualizing rapt audiences and effective presentations.

The Akashic Records, located on Level +03, serve as archives for all our prayers. The Records hold all our prayers and their answers. All of our life issues to date can be reviewed there.

Visualization is a key component to creating our life plans. Everyone visualizes. However, not everyone is aware of the power and ability of visualization, and some visualize without being conscious of it. Everyone is a creator, whether he or she knows it or not. It is our ability to create that makes us in God's image. It also places great responsibility on us, for we can choose to create heaven, or choose to create hell.

To visualize, create a picture in your mind of what you want to do, where you want to go, what you want to have. You may find writing words or images on paper make the effort more real. List your goals and the daily steps needed to reach each goal.

Some of you will cross off each step as you master it; others may put away the list and forget it's even there. You may also wish to create a ritual of vocalizing the image, of speaking it aloud. You can also combine writing, speaking, silently visualizing, and even cutting out photos or images to reinforce your picture. Your guides and angels are there to help you achieve your goals and dreams; you have but to ask.

Epilogue

I have presented my story with the help of my guides and angels. I offer it to you, the reader, in hopes that it may tear away the veil that surrounds our perceived reality and give you a small view of the "Big Picture." I do not seek to change your reality for that is yours. I wish to offer the reality that has been shown to me. I do my best to work in that reality. Part of the benefit for me in doing this writing is to present it in a hard copy and validate for myself that I experienced all these amazing adventures. I would want to spend all my time experiencing the extraterrestrial and no time living. I personally have to record this information, for to keep it all in my head and heart would render me of little use in this world.

I went to see the Counsel on the 30th level last night for I had some questions and had not been there in a long time. I asked Grandfather how it was that he was always there when I came to see him.

"Time," he said, "is not at all what you imagine it to be. It is circular. You may think of our existence as a fast-moving train traveling through the galaxies. Your thoughts bring you to the station where we stop and pick you up for a time. We then return you later to the station again." I thought that a very interesting analogy and wanted to include his words here in my closing words for you to mull over.

On a personal note I asked him why my vibrational status had shifted. He said my physical vessel was not ready yet for the higher vibration, for it would be like an engine rotating at too high a speed. He told me that in time, I would be able to tolerate the higher vibration. His words to me were, "Be patient." Gee, where had I heard that before?

The plan for me, in this lifetime, is to find a format that can reach as many people as possible. This is a time of change; the old is fading away. The new is fast upon us and we have agreed to be here for this change. Carter told me that I had eclectic taste. That is true, for I see beauty in all things: life, death, earth, space, every being has a uniqueness that is singular, one I find when I reach beyond the box. The light is brilliant. I can connect to rocks, vegetation, humans and star beings. The door is open to all possibility.

The revelations of hard times are now; we are living them. Change and rebirth come out of chaos. Take heart. The order that we seek is just beyond our view. The dark will pass away; it will implode within itself. Then the limitless light will guide the planet. We will have the opportunity to join other light beings in many galaxies to work through the problems we face in this techno-elitist destruction that has decimated the beautiful garden in which we have the blessing to live.

Ego-based fear is what the dark side uses to keep us fighting and fearing one another. When we can look beyond that deception and see the light of unconditional love for all of mankind, that is our salvation. Of course, the media will not like that turn of events for they feed on fear. That is why the headlines never say a miracle happened today. The same is true of government, which insists that we have an enemy; if non-existent, the government creates one.

Take heart. What would it cost to give up fear? Death, perhaps, but what is death? It is only a change of form we give up one vessel for another.

I ask that any of you who would: to please make a concerted effort to bring light to the dark world. That you understand that the vibration of the words we speak have ultimate power. God spoke this world into existence and we are in God's image. We have the power to speak the light into existence, for thought precedes action. Think of the garden and peace and light in the world, and it shall come to pass. Once you put that thought out to the Universe, the Universe will grant your request. Your thoughts and my thoughts make this reality. These same thoughts, yours and mine, can bring about a new reality: Heaven on Earth.

We are the light! Do not look to someone else to lead you. The God in you is the God in me. We are the God beings. We are one with the source. We are here, now, at this moment in time to manifest our God ship on this planet at this time. Now!

Blessed Be,

GINGER

Additional Resources, Reading and Contact Information

Recommended Reading:

Ageless Body, Timeless Mind by Deepak Chopra, MD

Angels A to Z by James R. Lewis and Evelyn D. Oliver

Emerging Viruses: AIDS and Ebola by Leonard G. Horowitz, DMD, MA, MPH

Hands of Light by Barbara Brennen

Healing Codes for the Biological Apocalypse
         by Leonard G. Horowitz, DMD, MA, MPH

Manifesting Your Heart's Desire by Fred Fengler and Todd Varnuor

Mayan Prophecies by Adrian G. Gilbert and Maurice M. Cotterell

The Celestine Prophecy by James Redfield

The Eagle and the Rose by Rosemary Altea

The Earth Chronicles by Zecharia Sitchin

The Future is Yours—Do Something With It by Raymond Grace

Urban Shaman by Serge Kyle King

Vibrational Medicine for the 21st Century by Robert Gerber, MD

GINGER—WHAT ABOUT Ellen kamhi and Traci Vandermark?

Contact Information:

Author: Ginger
Email: ginge54@iwon.com
www.level33ginger.com

Illustrator: Adam Henson
adamhenson@hotmail.com

Publisher: Goblin Fern Press
www.goblinfernpress.com
1-888-670-BOOK (2665)

Other valuable contact information:

John Kelly (shaman, healer) email: jkelly@cthealingarts.com

American Society of Dowsers email: ASD@dowsers.org,
web: www.dowsers.org

Astral Society: www.astralsociety.com

David E. Stanger: Tel: 1-819-843-8376

SomaEnergetics: www.SomaEnergetics.com

Cluster Water: 1-888-508-4787

BOOK ORDER FORM

(please copy and fill out)

To order your copy of *The Angel & the Alien* by Ginger, please provide the following information:

_____
Name

_____
Address

_____
City   State   Zip

_____
Email

_____
Phone

Quantity: _____ x $19.95: _____

Shipping & Handling: $4.50 for 1st book, $1 per book thereafter. Unless otherwise requested, books will be sent by USPS media mail.

S & H : _____

Subtotal: _____

If ordering from Wisconsin, please add 5.5% sales tax: _____

Order total: _____

Quantity discounts are available from the publisher.

Method of Payment   ☐ Check   ☐ Money Order   ☐ Visa

_____   _____   ☐ MasterCard
Credit Card #   Exp. date

☐ American Express

_____
Signature

Please copy this order form and send or fax with payment to:

Goblin Fern Press

3809 Mineral Point Road
Madison, WI 53705

Phone: 608-442-0212 / Fax: 608-442-0221
Toll-free: 888-670-BOOK (2665)
Email: info@goblinfernpress.com

Or order from our secure website:
www.GoblinFernPress.com

AAbkordf